W9-ARB-314

DINING WITH THE DEVIL

Praise for *Dining with the Devil*

"A timely indictment of a secularized evangelicalism that prizes success and worldly acclaim over theology and biblical fidelity."
—Donald Bloesch,
University of Dubuque Theological Seminary

"This is a very positive book! Its passion is to guard the church-growth movement so that it will also be a growth movement of God's Kingdom. Every evangelical Christian needs to understand how the devices of our modern age can affect our ministry."
—Paul Kooistra, President, Covenant Theological Seminary

"One would expect this book to be written 100 years from now by an historian looking at this generation in retrospect. Os Guinness has the rare ability to understand and interpret social trends even as they occur. He warns us that our uncritical embracing of modernity is destroying our ability to shape our lives around biblical truth. This threatens to render meaningless even our most gleaming models of success."
—Jim Petersen, The Navigators

"Os Guinness is pleading for God-centered, dolphin-like freedom for the sake of truth in the sea of modernity. He warns against the floating, jelly-fish tendencies of American evangelicalism. I have been mightily helped to swim against the tide, and to think 'against the world for the world.' "
—John Piper, Bethlehem Baptist Church, Minneapolis

"A genuine movement of God should be open to insight from its friendly critics, especially when such a critique is offered with the sort of spiritual and cultural insight given it here. Os Guinness helps all of us who are concerned about the American church's integrity and effectiveness."
—Joseph Ryan, Park Cities Presbyterian Church, Dallas

"Guinness shows the megachurch as dangerous to Christ's Church. . . Needs to be read."
—Arthur Taylor, former dean,
Fordham University's School of Business

OS GUINNESS

DINING WITH THE DEVIL

The Megachurch Movement Flirts with Modernity

HOURGLASS BOOKS

BAKER BOOK HOUSE
Grand Rapids, Michigan 49516

87558

© 1993 by Os Guinness

All rights reserved. No part of this book may be reproduced or transmitted in any form or by any means—electronic, mechanical, or otherwise, including photocopying—without written permission from the publisher, Hourglass Books, except for brief quotation in critical reviews or articles. Hourglass Books is an imprint of Baker Book House, P.O. Box 6287, Grand Rapids, MI 49516-6287.

A shortened, adapted version of this book appeared in *No God But God: Breaking With the Idols of Our Age*, Os Guinness and John Seel, eds. (Chicago: Moody Press, 1992).

"Fishers of Men" by Søren Kierkegaard, in *Kierkegaard's Attack Upon "Christendom" 1854–1855*, trans. Walter Lowrie, reprinted by permission. Copyright © 1944 by Princeton University Press.

"The Celestial Rail-road" by Nathaniel Hawthorne, in the *Centenary Edition of the Works of Nathaniel Hawthorne* published by the Ohio State University Center for Textual Studies and Ohio State University Press, reprinted by permission. Copyright © 1974 by the Ohio State University Press.

Scripture quotations taken from the *Holy Bible, New International Version*. Copyright © 1973, 1978, 1984 by International Bible Society.

ISBN 0-8010-3855-3

Printed in the United States of America

Cover by Eric Walljasper

Library of Congress Cataloging-in-Publication Data

Guinness, Os.
   Dining with the devil : the megachurch movement flirts with modernity / Os Guinness.
      p.   cm.
   Includes bibliographical references.
   ISBN 0-8010-3855-3
   1. Church growth—United States. 2. Big churches.
3. Christianity and culture. 4. United States—Church history—20th century. I. Title.
BR526.G85   1993
254'.5—dc20   93-16794

"He who sups with the devil had better have a long spoon. The devilry of modernity has its own magic: The [believer] who sups with it will find his spoon getting shorter and shorter—until that last supper in which he is left alone at the table, with no spoon at all and with an empty plate. The devil, one may guess, will by then have gone away to more interesting company."

— Peter L. Berger
A Rumor of Angels

CONTENTS

OPENING MEDITATION

FISHERS OF MEN
Søren Kierkegaard

THESE ARE CHRIST'S own words: "Follow me, and I will make you fishers of men." (Matthew 4:19).

So off went the Apostles.

But what was that likely to amount to, with these few men, who moreover understood Christ's words to mean that it was they who had to be sacrificed in order to catch men? It is easy to see that if things had gone on that way, it would have amounted to nothing. That was God's notion, perhaps a pretty one, but—as every practical man must surely admit—God is not practical. Or can one think of anything more topsy-turvy than that sort of fishing, where fishing means being sacrificed, so that it is not the fishermen who eat the fish but the fish who eat the fishermen? And that is what they call fishing! It is almost like Hamlet's madness when he says of Polonius that he is at a supper, not where he eats, but where he is eaten.

Then man undertook God's cause.

"Fishers of men! What Christ meant is something quite different from what these honest Apostles achieved, in defiance of all linguistic usage and linguistic analogy, for in no language is this what is understood by fishing. What He meant and intended was the origination of a new branch of business, i.e. man-fishery, preaching Christianity in such a way that it will amount to something to fish with this fishing company."

9

Attention now, and you will see that it does amount to something!

Yes, my word, it did amount to something! It amounted to "established Christendom" with millions and millions and millions of Christians.

It was quite simply arranged. Just as one company is formed to speculate in the herring-fishery, another in cod-fishing, another in whaling, etc., so man-fishing was carried on by a stock company which guaranteed its members a dividend of such and such a per cent.

And what was the result of it? If you haven't done it yet, don't fail to take advantage of this opportunity to admire man! The result was that they caught a prodigious number of herring, or what I mean is men, Christians; and of course the company was in a brilliant financial condition. It proved indeed that even the most successful herring company did not make nearly so big a profit as did man-fishery. And one thing further, an extra profit, or at least a piquant seasoning on top of the profit, namely, that no herring company is able to quote words of Scripture when they send boats out for the catch.

But man-fishery is a godly enterprise, the stockholders in this company can appeal to words of Scripture for themselves, for Christ says "I will make you fishers of men." They can tranquilly go to meet the Judgment, saying, "We have accomplished Thy word, we have fished for men."

INTRODUCTION

WHEN THE MALL OF AMERICA opened in Minneapolis in August 1992, enthusiasts hailed it as one of the seven wonders of the modern world. The largest, fully enclosed retail and entertainment complex in North America, its statistics were mind-boggling. It boasted enough floor space to fill eighty-eight football fields. It hired twice the number of workers employed by the city of Minneapolis. It anticipated 40 million annual visitors—nine times the population of Minnesota—and its first-year budget was twice that of the city of St. Paul. Nicknamed the "mega-mall" by Minnesotans, it drew screams, gasps, and tears from those who saw it for the first time.

But the strongest attraction of the new Mall of America was the "special services" that came with its four hundred shops. These included "Camp Snoopy," a seven-acre amusement park complete with a roller coaster, an eighteen-hole miniature golf course, numerous customer services, such as cellular phones for separated shoppers, and the ultimate special service—a church service in the rotunda between Bloomingdale's and Sears. "A Sunday Mallelujah!" cried the Minneapolis *Star Tribune* as six thousand flocked to the opening service organized by Wooddale Church of Eden Prairie.

Many people were enthusiastic. The service was one of the most enterprising and innovative they had ever seen. But others were shocked. A worship service no more has a place in a shopping mall than in a bar or a nightclub. My own view lies with the former, but both reactions missed a deeper point: The problem is not the presence of a church in a mall but the presence of the mall in the church.

The natural association of the megamall and the three-thousand-member megachurch was precisely what the pastors of Wooddale Church had in mind. The symbolism was perfect: Modern megachurches have been built on the philosophical and structural pattern of America's recent shopping malls, which, in turn, have long been described as "cathedrals of consumption." The local press described Wooddale Church as "a kind of megamall of suburban soulsaving." "Yes," said the pastor with a keen appreciation of his win-win relationship with the megamall, "We're going to bring the mall a lot of business. We've suggested to our people that they wear comfortable clothes in which to do any shopping they have in mind after lunch."[1]

Wooddale Church's initiative is an example of one of America's most prominent religious movements in the 1990s—"effective evangelism" through such modern means of "growing churches" as management, marketing, and megachurches. "Megachurch" has joined megabucks, megatrends, and the megamall as common American jargon. Megachurches, churches-for-the-unchurched with congregations over two thousand, are widely touted as "the inside track to fast growth" and a "leading trend of the coming millennium." The United States is now said to have over three hundred such megachurches—nearly fifty with over five thousand in attendance—and experts predict that five hundred will exist by A.D. 2000.

"One-stop shopping" is a theme common to all of the megachurches. The biggest offer not only spiritual attractions but such features as movie theaters, weight rooms, saunas, roller rinks, and racquetball courts. Once a growing church reaches the critical mass of one thousand, the sky is the limit for its financial and organizational potential for further growth through a myriad of dazzling modern insights and technologies.

The modern megachurches are a prominent new feature of the church-growth movement. Many people identify this movement narrowly with the specific architects and advocates of its earlier stages—most famously, Donald MacGavran, C. Peter Wagner, and the Charles E. Fuller Institute of Evangelism and Church Growth School. Others identify the movement with the most visible examples of its current success—most recently, such best-sellers as George Barna's *The Frog in the Kettle, Marketing The Church*, and *User-Friendly Churches*. But the burgeoning megachurches should be included too, epitomized by those on the "top ten" list, such as Garden Grove Community Church in southern California and Willow Creek Community Church in northwest suburban Chicago.

Thus as I use the term *church growth*, all these individuals and churches are part of a much wider and more important movement that is linked by a series of underlying commitments: to Christian renewal through renewal of the church, as opposed to politics or the culture; to renewal of the church through renewal of the local church, as opposed to the denomination or parachurch ministry; to the renewal of the local church through the renewal of mission, as opposed to other priorities; and, most importantly, to the renewal of mission along one of two avenues—through charismatic renewal or through the employment of the behavioral sciences' insights and tools to aid effective evangelism. In this final area, which is the focus of this critique, proponents use tools from the fields of management, marketing, psychology, and communications as they seek to "grow churches." Viewed in this broader way, the church-growth movement is a "back to basics" movement with a special modern twist.

The basic goals of the megachurches and the broader church-growth movement are laudable, ambitious, and significant for the church of Christ around the world. As C. Peter Wagner states them, they are "to make more effective the propagation of the gospel and the multiplication of churches *on new ground*" and thus to "seeing America evangelized in our generation."[2]

Leaving aside for the moment the unexplained "new ground," no follower of Christ can quarrel with this basic purpose. But can the movement attain these goals? Will it change the landscape of American religion? Will its passion for mission and effective evangelism lead to a harvest of new Christians and reverse the secularization of the West? Will its innovations amount to a reformation in the worldwide church? Can the secrets of successful megachurches be carried over to struggling small churches?

Like most Christians, my own response to these questions would be a heartfelt prayer of support. But in our enthusiasm we must not be swept away and forget to ask two more important questions. What is the church-growth movement's so-called "new ground"? And are most proponents of church growth and the megachurches even aware of how "new ground" influences the movement?

This book is a constructive critique of the church-growth movement and the new megachurches, focusing especially on the use of this "new ground" of modern insights and techniques. Any movement that simultaneously hits *Time*, *Newsweek*, and *Christianity Today* and is viewed by so many Christian leaders as the best remedy for the church's ineffectiveness in the modern world deserves to be noticed, understood, and assessed.

My purpose is not to dismiss this vital movement, or even to assess it comprehensively from a theological perspective, but to critique the perils and pitfalls that come from the "new ground." There will be no name calling or mud-slinging in this critique. My approach is to examine trends, raise issues, and set out principles so that we may engage with this vital movement with our eyes open and our ears alert, being as self-critical and discerning as the gospel requires.

Of course, I am aware that at the end of the day what I think about the church-growth movement or anything else matters little. What really matters is what God thinks. For the day is coming when we will either hear "Well done," and our work will prove to be "gold and silver." Or, we will be judged by the test of fire and our work shown up as "wood, hay, and stubble." Or, worst of all, we may hear the terrible words, "I never knew you" and find ourselves, as C. S. Lewis put it, "banished from the presence of him who is present everywhere and erased from the knowledge of him who knows all."[3]

Followers of Christ, then, should consider all serious criticism because openness to correction is a matter of Christian principle. But finally only one audience matters—the audience of one. All other judgments will themselves be judged by the judgments of that Grand Assize.

MODERNITY AND THE SEARCH FOR LOST AUTHORITY

The rise and implications of the megachurch movement need to be understood in the setting of the global challenge of modernity. The historic and stirring events of 1989 in Eastern Europe and the former Soviet Union raise critical issues about the central challenge to faith in our time—faith's loss of authority under the impact of the modern world, and thus of its need to recover integrity and effectiveness. Much ink has flowed to say what the European revolution and "the second Russian revolution" mean for Western liberal democracy, but less on their significance for the gospel.

A complete analysis of these recent events is beyond our purpose here, but one part is highly relevant to faith and the church-growth movement: the influence of modernity. Modernity, which is the factor overlooked in the Soviet crisis, is a key to both the crisis in America and the crisis within the church, to which the church-growth movement is the proposed solution.

Seen from this perspective, the European revolution was a triumph for both liberal democracy and faith, although the triumph was not complete for either. The year 1989 represented a stunning vindication of two of the three spheres of the American republic—it was a triumph for America's political order, epitomizing representative democracy, and for America's economic order, epitomizing democratic capitalism. Liberal democracy is now less rivaled than at any time in our century.

But the third great sphere that makes up the American republic's tripartite order—the moral and cultural sphere—is in deep trouble. At the very moment of her historic political and economic vindication, a crisis of cultural authority is sapping the very vitality of the United States. Americans are no longer shaped by beliefs, ideals, and traditions as they once were. It is now questionable whether America's cultural order is capable of nourishing the freedom, responsibility, and civility that Americans require to sustain democracy.

America's crisis of cultural authority is larger than this one point, but at its heart is a crisis of religious and civic faith rooted in the impact of modernity. Compared with the past, faith today influences culture less. Compared with the past, culture today influences faith more. Under the impact of modernity, which has contributed so much to the undoing of Marxism in the Soviet Union, America's own civic and religious beliefs have lost much of their "binding address."

I am not suggesting any "moral equivalence" between the USA and the former USSR. The differences are all important— and not least that of their two dominant faiths the gospel is true and Marxism is false. But both crises result in part from modernity's impact on the ideas, beliefs, and traditions of each society.

Put simply, modernity can be understood as the character and system of the world produced by the forces of development and modernization, especially capitalism, industrialized technology, and telecommunications. The impact of modernity in the United States means that the Christian faith has lost much of its integrity and effectiveness in shaping the lives of believers. The statistical indicators of faith are still high, but its social influence is down. A central fact of modern times is faith's search for its own lost authority. A central challenge of modern times is faith's need to recover its integrity and effectiveness.

Christian integrity and effectiveness are never easy, but the challenge is made more difficult today by this altogether new factor—the global and all-encompassing reality of modernity. Unless we address the challenge of modernity, we overlook, to our peril, both the setting in which the search for lost authority is taking place and the scale of the challenge. The following twelve statements summarize the basic components of this challenge.

1. *Modernity is the central fact of human life today:* Modernity is the first truly global culture in the world and the most powerful culture in history so far. Thus the empire of modernity is the great alternative to the kingdom of God. Extensively, it encircles the planet; intensively, it encompasses more and more of each individual's life. The massiveness and seeming permanence of its imperial systems and ideology threaten us with captivity as surely as the empire of Egypt did Moses and the empires of Assyria and Babylon did exiled Israel.

2. *Modernity is double-edged for human beings:* Modernity simultaneously represents the greatest human advances in history—in such benefits as health, speed, power, and convenience—and the greatest assaults on humanness in history—in such areas as the crisis of identity and the crisis of the family.

3. *Modernity is double-edged for followers of Christ:* Modernity represents the crux of the contemporary challenge to the gospel because it is the greatest single opportunity and the greatest single challenge the church has faced since the apostles. In the first case, it is equivalent of Roman roads in the first century and printing presses in the sixteenth. In the second, it is our equivalent of the challenges of persecution and gnosticism rolled into one.

4. *Modernity is foundational for the character and identity of both Americans and American evangelicals:* The United States as the world's "first new nation" and American evangelicalism as Protestantism's "first new tradition" both have features of modernity that are constitutive of their very character and identity (for example, pluralism in the case of America and a reliance on technique in the case of evangelicalism). This close affinity is an advantage because America and American evangelicalism

have prospered at the growing edge of modernity. But it is also a disadvantage in a double sense: those most blessed by modernity are most blind to it, and those first hit by modernity are often the worst hurt by modernity. This is one reason why non-Westerners in relation to Americans, and Roman Catholics and Orthodox in relation to evangelicals, consider themselves superior to, and immune from, either the crises facing America or American evangelicals.

5. *Modernity's central challenge to America is focused in America's crisis of cultural authority:* Modernity creates problems far deeper than drugs, crime, illiteracy, AIDS, broken families, or the plight of the inner cities. It creates a crisis of cultural authority in which America's beliefs, ideals, and traditions are losing their compelling power in society. What people believe no longer makes much difference to how they behave. Unless reversed, this hollowing out of beliefs will finally be America's undoing.

6. *Modernity's central challenge to evangelicals is focused in the crisis of the authority of faith:* Modernity undermines the churches' capacity both to demonstrate the integrity and effectiveness of faith and to provide an answer to America's crisis. Their captivity to modernity is the reason why faith's influence on the culture has decreased while culture's influence on faith has increased.

7. *Modernity is a monumental paradox to the everyday practice of faith:* Modernity simultaneously makes evangelism easier—more people at more times in their lives are more open to the gospel—yet makes discipleship harder, because practicing the lordship of Christ runs counter to the fragmentation and specialization of modern life.

8. *Modernity pressures the church toward polarized responses:* Ever since the early days of modernity in the eighteenth century, a pattern of response to modernity has grown strong. Liberals have generally tended to surrender to modernity without criticizing it; conservatives have tended to defy modernity without understanding it. This tendency has been reversed in the last generation as more progressive evangelicals now court the

"affluent consumers" of the gospel as ardently as liberals once courted the "cultured despisers" of the gospel. The two main examples today are the megachurch leaders marrying the managerial, as we shall see, and the Christian publishers romancing the therapeutic.

9. *Modernity's challenge cannot be escaped by the common responses to which Christians typically resort:* Those who recognize the deficiencies of the extreme liberal and conservative responses often go onto two further deficient responses. One is a resort to premodernism—looking to the Third World to refresh the West, not realizing that Third World Christians have yet to face the inevitable challenge of modernization. This is true too of our brothers and sisters in Eastern Europe and Russia, who face a greater challenge from modernity than they previously faced from Marxism. The other is the resort to postmodernism—failing to see that though modernism as a set of ideas built on the Enlightenment has collapsed, modernity, as the fruit of capitalism and industrialized technology, is stronger than ever.

10. *Modernity represents a special challenge to the church:* The three strongest national challenges to the gospel in the modern world are Japan, Europe, and the United States. Japan has never been won to Christ; Europe has been won twice and lost twice; and America, though having the strongest and wealthiest churches, is now experiencing the severest crisis, so represents the clearest test case of Christian responses to modernity.

11. *Modernity represents a special challenge to reformation:* The reason for this special challenge is its central dismissal of the place of words. On the one hand, the overwhelming thrust of modernity has been to replace words with images and reading with viewing. On the other hand, the words that remain have been weakened because they have become technical, specialized, and abstract to most people. At the same time, postmodernism further devalues words by using them to create a pastiche of effect regardless of their original meaning (for example, the multiple cultural uses of "born-again" in advertising or news programs).

12. *Modernity represents a special challenge to revival:* Quite simply, it is a fact of history that the church of Christ has not experienced any major nationwide revival under the conditions of advanced modernity. On the one hand, modernity undercuts true dependence on God's sovereign awakening by fostering the notion that we can effect revival by human means. On the other hand, modernity makes many people satisfied with privatized, individualistic, and subjective experiences that are pale counterfeits of true revival. While many Christians no longer have a practical expectation of revival, those who count on God's sovereignty over modernity have every reason to look to God for revival once again.

SPOTLIGHT ON THE NEW GROUND

This emphasis on the challenge of modernity is not as odd as it may seem. America's crisis of cultural authority and the global challenge of modernity provide the setting and underscore the significance of the church-growth movement and the megachurches. For the church-growth movement is one of the church's most deliberate and important responses to the crisis of authority of faith in modern culture. (Other prominent but less laudable responses are the resort to the therapeutic revolution or to a politicized faith.)

To be sure, many church-growth advocates see the church's problem simply as a matter of out-of-date structures and out-of-touch communication, which can all be remedied easily. This naïveté trivializes a crisis that is far more massive than they realize. But it is not surprising that when the church, and its ministers and their preaching, are all widely perceived as "irrelevant" in the modern world, such a resort to new forms of authority and relevance appears justified as well as necessary.

Doubtless, this emphasis on modernity does appear odd. For a start, the roots of the church-growth movement are surely in the Third World and thus far from the late twentieth-century world of the West—after all, the movement rose out of Donald MacGavran's missionary work in India in the 1930s. But the movement has now moved beyond its original missionary phase and even its early American phase. The church-growth movement has come into its own in a third phase, through the highly popularized form of the megachurches, which have everything to do with modernity.

Beyond that, it must also seem a little excessive to critique the church-growth movement with the global category of modernity—an exercise that is rather like using a sledgehammer to crack a peanut. But in fact the whole importance of the movement's third phase lies in the two little words "new ground." The meaning of the third phase can be seen at the point where the movement's "new ground" intersects with the challenge of modernity and the church's search to reclaim lost authority. Modernity, like the empire of Egypt that Moses faced, is so massive and strong that nothing short of the power of the true gospel can prevail over it. So any movement that steps forward to champion Christian renewal in the setting of modernity soon discovers that it confronts the ultimate challenge: modernity's exposure of its character and strength. Is it the genuine article or not?

This fateful exposure by modernity of the megachurch movement's "new ground" is the nub of the argument of this book. In short, the argument is that the megachurch movement is flirting dangerously with modernity. Or, more prosaically, that church growth on the basis of the church-growth movement's "new ground" is no answer to the crisis of modernity because the use of the "new ground" itself is an uncritical accommodation to modernity. Far from leading to an exodus, modern church growth often uses the ideology and tools of Egypt to make the life of the people of God more comfortable in captivity.

THE MOVEMENT OF THE 1990S

In this assessment of the megachurch and church-growth movement, it is important to say that the movement as a whole has an immensely positive spiritual, cultural, and historical significance for the church of Christ. These positive aspects of church growth must not be ignored.

First, spiritually, the church-growth movement represents a concern for many of the most-needed components of Christian mission, renewal, and reformation. This can be seen by stressing the movement's most obvious emphases—the centrality of the church, the priority of mission, the possibility of growth, the necessity of speaking to outsiders, the acknowledgment of culture and of cultures, the insistence on real results, and the wisdom of using the best insights and technologies proffered by the key disciplines of the human sciences.

Second, culturally, the church-growth movement represents the most influential movement in the American churches in the 1990s, and a significant expression of the search for the lost authority of faith. The church-growth movement and the Christian Right are only two of many movements within the wider Christian community. But the contrast between their respective standings in the early eighties and the early nineties tells the story of the cultural shifts that have occurred from one decade to the next. For all the sustained activism of Operation Rescue and the talk of a new conservative political party, the Christian Right is largely a spent force; the shift to the centrality of local churches is therefore both vital and illuminating.

Ten years ago the attention was on the Christian Right; today it is on church growth. Then the cry was "Mobilize!"; now it's "Modernize!" Then the focus was politics and public life; now it is church and mission. Then the reliance was on populism and political strength; now it is on entrepreneurialism and managerial strength. Then the orientation was the past and the restoration of the nineteenth-century consensus; now it is the future and renewal. Then the attention was on special-interest groups, epitomized by the Moral Majority; now it is on the megachurches.

These cultural and spiritual shifts are enormously important. So long as the United States remains the world's lead society, it represents the advancing storm front of modernity, and modernity's impact on the world of faith. American followers of Christ should therefore stand and prevail to recover the full integrity and effectiveness of the gospel. How the church-growth movement fares in its proclaimed mission will therefore be both important and instructive.

Third, historically, the church-growth movement is a significant new initiative in the long story of Christian innovation and adaptation. In essence, it is the most significant attempt by the conservative churches in North America to grope toward a new stance in a society that has sidelined the Christian faith and become increasingly secular in its public life and pluralistic in its private life.

Curiously, this fact is easily overlooked because of the movement's own rhetoric of accusation. Church-growth leaders speak and write so much about Christians and churches who are "hidebound," "stuck-in-the-mud," or "dying for change" that people come to take their attacks as descriptions. "Frankly," one author writes without a sense of historical perspective, "evangelical Christianity has done well on revelation (the Bible) but poorly on relevance (the culture)."[4] This gives the impression of a Neanderthal church incapable of change.

Certainly, stories of diehard resistance to change are easy to find. But the Christian faith is unrivaled among the world religions for its genius in innovation and adaptation. And no branch of the Christian faith has demonstrated this genius more often and more successfully than the evangelical movement.

All innovation is open to question and different assessments. And the darker side of this innovative genius is the church's proneness to compromise with the spirit of its age. But from the adaptations of the early church—for example, Augustine's translations of the language and ideas of Platonism down to the innovations of eighteenth-century Methodism and nineteenth-century revivalism—Christians have been tirelessly determined to innovate and adapt for the sake of the gospel.

The wise use of modernity's insights and technologies could therefore lead to one of the most fruitful periods of innovation in the church's two-thousand-year history. The managerial revolution, for example, could provide the church with a large, varied, and powerful toolbox. To some people, the term "manage" has a sinister ring of manipulation—not least because of the "scientific paternalism" of early management studies and because it came into the English language from the Italian *maneggiare*, which means "to train, or handle, horses." But that is unfair. After all, the core theme of management is essentially the biblical principle of stewardship, whether of people, resources, or time.

Many Christians have shown a great flair for management—John Wesley's nickname in the Holy Club in Oxford was "the manager" and the same brilliance in organization and personal discipline is what gave the Methodists their name.

Many other Christians have fruitfully employed such categories as Jesus' "new wine" and "new wineskins" long before anyone talked of "paradigm revolutions." They have not realized how close they were to the management of change. Today, in fact, many Christians abuzz with Thomas Kuhn's jargon forget that the notion comes directly from the Christian understanding of conversion. Since conversion is the ultimate paradigm revolution, Christians should not reduce the notion by misapplying it to trivial change.

In sum, innovation is not a problem. If Christians were to use the best fruits of the managerial revolution constructively and critically, accompanied by a parallel reformation of truth and theology, the potential for the gospel would be incalculable.

Whatever criticisms need to be raised, this point is beyond dispute: The church-growth movement is extraordinarily influential and significant within American churches today. At its best, it should be applauded. Where it is not at its best, it requires criticism so that it might be. The church of Christ concerned for the glory of Christ needs more—not less—of the best of true church growth.

WEAKNESSES TO WATCH

Like many movements, the church-growth movement is a grand mixture of things good, bad, and in-between. I will not comment further on its good parts—except to say that anything that "goes without saying" is in danger of being left unsaid. The best of the church-growth movement deserves better than that.

Our present concern, however, is not the good but rather the bad and the in-between elements, and in particular the range of problems that grow from the movement's uncritical use of such insights and tools of modernity as management and marketing. Obviously, size itself is not the problem with church growth. Some of the most celebrated churches in Christian history have been enormous—for example, Charles Haddon Spurgeon's Metropolitan Tabernacle in nineteenth-century London regularly drew more than ten thousand worshipers. Size, however, is a critical factor in opening up a church to the temptations of modernity. For, as stressed earlier, once a church reaches the critical mass of one thousand its financial and organizational potential for growth becomes great, but so also does its entanglement with modernity.

Obviously, too, not all of these criticisms apply equally to all large churches or to all church-growth proponents and some do not apply at all. All criticisms therefore come with an "If the shoe fits. . ." proviso. Many church-growth proponents, for example, are wilder in their rhetoric than in their reality, just as many church-growth excesses are more exaggerated in their copycat disciples than in the original churches from which they were cloned.

Although if the movement has a threefold positive significance, it also has a fourfold weakness. First, the very name, "church-growth movement," is confusing because both words are capable of a double meaning. On the one hand, does the term *church* refer to "the people of God," including all the people of God in a local area, or to a particular local church and its facility and programs? The two are not necessarily the same. If the distinction is not kept clear, the admirable growth in the first sense can be used to cover a less admirable growth in the second, which actually hurts the first. One example is when it leads to an essentially consumerist competition between particular local churches that simultaneously thrusts up superchurches and impoverishes other churches and the overall work of God in a local area.

On the other hand, is the term *growth* to be understood quantitatively, in terms of size and numbers, or qualitatively, in terms of depth, character, and spirit? Both sorts of growth are essential to the church, and qualitative growth does not exclude quantifiable growth. But nor does the quantitative growth exhaust qualitative growth. To pretend otherwise through careless use of the terms is a cardinal error of modern times and a fallacy in much church-growth rhetoric. Sometimes the difference is difficult to see. All too often it is easy. As one megachurch pastor boasted about his church to the *Wall Street Journal*, "It is the fastest growing church" in the nation. "I want the biggest church I can think of."[5]

Second, the church-growth movement has two common deficiencies. On the one hand, its theological understanding is often superficial, with almost no element of biblical criticism. As a well-known proponent states, "I don't deal with theology. I'm simply a methodologist"—as if his theology were thereby guaranteed to remain critical and his methodology neutral. Obviously there are distinguished exceptions to this criticism. It is also true that theology figured much more prominently in the early days of the movement, when there were solid grounds for assuming unspoken biblical commitments. But the present stage of the movement is extremely different, and no amount of charity can excuse it. Today theology is rarely more than marginal in the church-growth movement at the popular level. Discussion of the traditional marks of the church is virtually nonexistent. Instead, methodology is at the center and in control. The result is a methodology only occasionally in search of a theology. After all, Church Growth, as opposed to church growth, is a self-professed "science," not a theology.

The present critique focuses primarily on the errors in methodology that result from church-growth's naive reliance on modernity's "new ground." But the even more important theological critique remains to be done. For example, what of the megachurches' subordination of worship and discipleship to evangelism, and all three to entertainment, a problem that is already the Achilles' heel of evangelicalism? Or in evangelism itself, what of the foundational maxim that "a healthy church will grow numerically"? Unless critiqued theologically, that maxim can slide from a proper emphasis on a healthy church presenting the gospel to unbelievers to an improper emphasis on the health of a church being judged according to unbelievers' response to the gospel. Who, after all, is really giving the increase? Who is responsible for the response? Methodologically, the answers to these questions make little difference. A church grows either way. But theologically, they mean the difference between church growth as true faith and church growth as a form of streamlined humanistic engineering.

On the other hand, the second common deficiency is that the church-growth movement—true to its American evangelical parentage—displays a minimal sense of historical awareness. It is particularly unaware of comparisons with earlier periods that could throw light on the possibilities and pitfalls we face today. Two periods, for example, would give fruitful parallels: the late eighteenth century and the story of European liberalism's engagement with the "cultured despisers," and the early nineteenth century and the story of American evangelicalism's fateful sea-change during the era of Jacksonian populism. This early nineteenth-century change is a particularly important precedent because it was not so much from Calvinism to Arminianism as from theology to experience, from truth to technique, from elites to populism, and from an emphasis on "serving God" to an emphasis on "servicing the self" in serving God.[6]

Third, the church-growth movement has two common flaws through which the confusions and deficiencies mentioned above become more serious. On the one hand, it employs a lopsided application of a biblical principle. Known technically as "contextualization," or more simply as "relevance," this principle is indispensable to communication and obviously rooted in Scripture. The supreme pattern of the "contextualization" and "relevance" is the incarnation of God in Jesus Christ. Such passages as 1 Corinthians 9:19–22 capture its full dynamic perfectly, climaxing in Paul's summary: "I have become all things to all men so that by all possible means I might save some."

Thus the record of Scripture and Christian history is equally clear: the principle of identification is basic to communication and is covered well today in such notions as "contextualization" and "relevance," as well as in such church-growth principles as "niche marketing," "audience-driven," "seeker-friendly," "full-service churches," and the "homogeneous unit principle." The latter is otherwise known as "the birds of a feather" principle, and many church-growth advocates use it with consummate sartorial savvy: "Use a penny loafer to evangelize a penny loafer. It works. An Air Jordan might intimidate and a wingtip confuse a penny loafer, but another penny loafer may well communicate."[7]

But Scripture and history are also clear: Without maintaining critical tension, the principle of identification is a recipe for compromise and capitulation. It is no accident that the charge of being "all things to all people" has become a popular synonym for compromise. If the process of becoming "all things to all people" is to remain faithful to Christ, it has to climax in clear persuasion and profound conversion. Joining people where they are is only the first step in the process, not the last. Unless it resists this danger, the megachurch and church-growth movement will prove to be a gigantic exercise in cultural adjustment and surrender.

The very reason why penny loafers speak better to other penny loafers than to Air Jordans and wingtips is the reason why a penny-loafer gospel will never be the whole counsel of God. Put differently, "all things to all people" means it is perfectly legitimate to convey the gospel in cartoons to a non-literary generation incapable of rising above MTV and *USA Today*. But five years later, if the new disciples are truly won to Christ, they will be reading and understanding Paul's letter to the Romans and not simply the Gospel According to Peanuts.

On the other hand—and here is the main doorway to the dangers under discussion—many in the movement employ an uncritical understanding of modernity and its insights and tools. "Truth is truth," as George Macdonald put it, "whether from the lips of Jesus or Balaam."[8] It would therefore be odd for any Christian to deny the illuminating helpfulness of the social sciences. At the same time, however, it is amazing to witness the lemming-like rush of church leaders who forget theology in the charge after the latest insights of sociology—regardless of where the ideas come from or where they lead to. Carelessly handled, innovation and adaptation become a form of corruption, capitulation, and idolatry.

Fourth, the church-growth movement carries two potential dangers. They can be summed up simply in the words "no God" and "no grandchildren." In the first case, the problem results because the insights and tools of modernity can be so brilliant and effective that there no longer appears to be any need for God. In the second case, the problem arises because the tools of modernity are successful in one generation but cannot be sustained to the third generation. The success undermines the succession.

Many superchurches are simply artificially inflated local churches with charismatically inflated super-pastors that will not be able to survive their supergrowth. After all, the grand and gleaming megamalls will soon become an anachronism themselves and so will the megachurches that have copied them. At least the Catholics can justify St. Peter's, Rome by the papacy and the Vatican behind it. Third generation superchurches, by contrast, will have only their size and earlier success, with no claim to papal authority or catholic universality to sustain them.

In short, through these weaknesses and above all through its uncritical use of the "new ground" of modernity, the church-growth and megachurch movement has the potential to unleash a deadly form of idolatry and practical atheism in the churches. The result would be one more contemporary testament to the extraordinary power of religion that has no need for God.

A LONG SPOON AND A HAMMER

Critical discernment is necessary for all who appreciate the promise and the peril of the megachurch and church-growth movement. What follows are seven major reminders to help cultivate that critical discernment. Before we explore these seven reminders, however, we will turn to three preliminary considerations that have shaped these reminders.

First, Christians tend to fall into two equal and opposite errors when thinking of new movements, such as church growth. One is to applaud a new movement simply because it is new and it works—in this case adopting church growth as the beginning and end of contemporary renewal. The other error is to dismiss it because it is modern and it works. Thus, curiously, the first reaction accepts the church-growth movement without a qualm and the second attacks it without question—but both for the same reason. This contradictory response proves the need for discernment almost by itself.

In contrast, this essay seeks to raise a word of caution and offer tools for critical discernment—to ensure that the baby and the bathwater each end up where they should.

Second, two fundamental categories should shape all of our thinking and living as believers, especially our use of the world's gifts and benefits. One is the New Testament insistence that disciples of Christ are to be "in the world, but not of it," or—to put the emphasis on time rather than space—that we are *no longer* what we were before we came to Christ, but *not yet* what we will be when Christ returns.

The other critical category comes from the early church's application of this principle, based on the story of the exodus. Origen, in the third century A.D., taught that Christians are free to "plunder the Egyptians" but forbidden to "set up a golden calf" from the spoils. "In/not of," "no longer/not yet," "free to utilize/forbidden to idolize"—each contrast expresses the critical tension with the world that we are required to maintain. This tension is simultaneously a sign of obedience and a source of strength, a leading distinctive and a leading dynamic. It is what makes Christians the world's "resident aliens" (Augustine). It is what puts us in the challenging position of being "against the world for the world" (The Hartford Declaration).

Third, two useful pictures of what it means to develop critical discernment should challenge Christians. One, which is behind the title of this book, comes from the Christian social scientist, Peter Berger, a renowned analyst of modernity. He warns that whoever sups with the devil of modernity had better have a long spoon. "The devilry of modernity has its own magic." The believer "who sups with it will find his spoon getting shorter and shorter—until that last supper in which he is left alone at the table, with no spoon at all and with an empty plate."[9] Our challenge, then, is to dine at the banquet of modernity—but with long spoons.

The other picture comes from Friedrich Nietzsche's *The Twilight of the Idols*. In words that are more biblical than he intended, he wrote, "There are more idols in the world than there are realities." Our task, then, is to "sound out idols," to "pose questions with a hammer," to be iconoclasts, and see whether many of the things taken for granted in our time are in fact hollow, not real—mere "idols of the age."[10]

DISCERNMENT MAKES A DIFFERENCE

Is it possible to achieve critical discernment that makes a practical difference in engaging with the church-growth movement? Definitely—once the point of the seven reminders is appreciated. Take two types of possible applications. One concerns the exercise of discernment in *assessing modern insights*. Lack of discernment here often prevents Christians from noticing crucial shifts in logic: from *is* to *ought,* from *description* to *prescription,* and most commonly from statements of *description* ("This is the way modern people are. . .") to statements of *explanation* ("This is why modern people are the way they are. . .") and statements of *solution* ("This is the way to deal with modern people because of the way they are. . .").

Such shifts are critically important because modern insights are usually at their most perceptive and most useful to Christians when they are at the level of description. The Christian view, however, usually begins to differ from modern views significantly when there is a shift to the level of explanation. By the same token, modern answers are usually at their least helpful, if not most dangerous, when they are at the level of solution. In failing to recognize these shifts, many Christians also fail to notice the dangers until too late. They do not realize that the logic of the solution is implied in the logic of the explanation.

The other type of application concerns the exercise of discernment in *employing modern insights and tools.* The challenge here is to stop the idolizing of good and useful things. Contrary to popular misconceptions, idols in the Bible are not simply the concerns of others ("pagans") and their obvious objects of worship ("gods of wood and stone"). In the biblical view, anything created—anything at all that is less than God, and most especially the gifts of God—can become idolatrous if it is relied upon inordinately until it becomes a full-blown substitute for God and, thus, an idol that takes the place of God.

In the case of the church-growth movement, this idolizing trend can develop in one of two ways: either the insights and tools of modernity are themselves relied upon idolatrously, or the churches themselves become idolatrous because their very success as institutions makes them into an end in themselves.

We should therefore be on the lookout for the idolizing of good things and be prepared to assess the use of the best insights and tools. On the one hand, in searching for the best, we should ask: where are modern insights and tools *legitimate* and *fruitful?* (Because all truth is God's truth, we are free to plunder.) On the other hand, in looking out for the worst, we should ask: where are modern insights and tools *double-edged*? (Because they contain negative and positive aspects, unintended and intended consequences.) Where are they *excessive*? (Because useful though they may be, it is possible to trust in them inordinately, making them either unbalanced or unbounded.) Where are they *autonomous*? (Because their very brilliance and effectiveness encourages us to treat them separately from other moral, human, and theological considerations.) And, finally, where are they *idolatrous*? (Not because the insights and tools are inherently evil, but because—through their very usefulness—they can be points of false reliance and even working substitutes for God.)

We now turn to look at seven reminders that will help cultivate critical discernment and help avoid idolatry in the megachurch movement's engagement with modernity. The best of the movement will doubtless pass through unscathed. Much of the rest requires tougher scrutiny than most Christians are now giving it.

Questions for Reflection and Discussion

1. What do you see as the crisis in the church or culture to which the church-growth movement is perceived as the effective remedy?

2. What are the pros and cons of the megachurch and church-growth movement as you know it?

3. Do the examples of the church-growth movement that you have encountered illustrate the better or worse features of the movement?

1

ONE MAIN QUESTION

WHEN ALL IS SAID AND DONE, the church-growth movement will stand or fall by one question. In implementing its vision of church growth, is the church of Christ primarily guided and shaped by its own character and calling—or by considerations and circumstances alien to itself? Or, to put the question differently, is the church of Christ a social reality truly shaped by a theological cause, namely the Word and Spirit of God? In sum, what—in practice—is the church's decisive authority?

Behind this question lies the fact that the church of God "lets God be God" and is the church only when she lives and thrives finally by God's truths and God's resources. If the church makes anything else the decisive principle of her existence, Christians risk living unauthorized lives of faith, exercising unauthorized ministries, and proclaiming an unauthorized gospel.

Yet, that is precisely the temptation modernity gives to us. The very brilliance and power of its tools and insights mean that eventually God's authority is no longer decisive. There is no longer quite the same need to let God be God. In fact, there is no need for God at all in order to achieve extraordinary measurable success. Thus, modernity creates the illusion that, when God commanded us not to live by bread alone but by every word that comes from his mouth, he was not aware of the twentieth century. The very success of modernity may undercut the authority and driving power of faith until religion becomes

35

merely religious rhetoric or organizational growth without spiritual reality.

BEWARE MODERNITY BEARING GIFTS

"Let my people go!" Those four bare words of the LORD confronted and overcame the empire of Egypt in the battle between God and the gods. And likewise today a showdown is staged between those for whom the decisive authority in life is modernity's imperial ideology and technology and those for whom it is God's sovereign freedom and the primacy of words and the Word. Words and speech, say the former, are as light as air. What counts is the solidity of programs, data, results, and the bottom line. Words and speech, say the latter, create and order realities decisively. Even miracles are only "signs" of the authority of the words spoken. Without speech, there is only the captivity and death of managed reality. Only with truth-filled speech is there life, hope, and freedom.

Needless to say, the issue is not God or modernity, as if God's sovereignty and modernity, or Christian orthodoxy and contemporary relevance, were mutually exclusive. The issue, instead, is which one is the decisive authority in practice. And the answer to that question is far more than a theological abstraction. For just as some Christians need reminding that they will not prove relevant unless they prove orthodox, so others need reminding that they do not truly know the sovereignty of God unless they know it in the setting of its greatest challenge today—modernity. For Christians of both types, the nub of the matter is this: The secret of both the difference of the church and the difference that the church hopes to make is the difference of God.

Put differently, the biblical view of how to use God's gifts—such as the gifts of modernity—without idolizing them requires two elements. First, the giver must be in the gift and, second, the receiver must know and receive the giver in the gift. As George Macdonald said, "No gift unrecognized as coming from God is at its own best."[1] When we recognize these requirements, we find God in all his gifts and in him find all things. But when we do not, God's own gifts become idols. And no one is more against his own gifts when idolized than God.

Put differently again, modernity is a colossal accentuation of a deep cleavage in the human soul that is as old as the Fall but is widened and unhealed since Sinai. As sinful human beings we have an instinctual, compulsive bias toward forms of religion that we ourselves can create and control. In particular we are lured toward the fertile and varied forms of polytheism rather than the bare finality of monotheism—or "monototheism" as Nietzsche satirized it—and toward images, or the representation of presence in figured form, rather than words. In short, nothing "meets our needs" like need-meeting gods in our own image.

At Sinai, however, God revealed himself as the all-decisive Other, the one God who cannot be played off against other gods or even against his own gifts that are given his place. And he revealed himself as a God beyond human imagining who spoke in words beyond human images. Abrupt, final, terrifying, unrelenting, the all-decisive Word of the all-demanding God confronts our natural reversions to forms of religion that our human senses can grasp, control, and find comfortable.

In light of this biblical view of gifts and the awesome but forbidding challenge at the heart of Sinai, it is curious that the church-growth movement's "new ground"—its use of modernity—is one of its most prominent but least examined features. This first reminder therefore deals with the first and greatest problem modernity poses for the megachurch movement—because it appears to be no problem at all.

Modernity is most dangerous at its best—not its worst—when its benefits and blessings are unarguable. No civilization in history has offered more gifts and therefore has amplified the temptation of living "by bread alone" with such power and variety and to such effect. In today's convenient, climate-controlled spiritual world created by the managerial and therapeutic revolutions, nothing is easier than living apart from God. Idols are simply the ultimate techniques of human causation and control—without God. God's sovereign freedom has met its match in ours. We have invented the technology to put God's Word on hold.

One Florida pastor with a seven-thousand-member megachurch expressed the fallacy well: "I must be doing right or things wouldn't be going so well."[2] One Christian advertising agent, who both represented the Coca-Cola Corporation and engineered the "I Found It" evangelistic campaign, paraded his golden calf brazenly: "Back in Jerusalem where the church started, God performed a miracle there on the day of Pentecost. They didn't have the benefits of buttons and media, so God had to do a little supernatural work there. But today, with our technology, we have available to us the opportunity to create the same kind of interest in a secular society." Put simply, another church-growth consultant claims, "five to ten million baby boomers would be back in the fold within a month" if churches adopted three simple changes: 1. "Advertise" 2. Let people know about "product benefits" 3. Be "nice to new people."[3]

"Beware modernity bearing gifts." This warning should not be confused with the superspiritual fallacy that flatters the church as being purely spiritual and theological, turning up its nose at all lesser, "unspiritual" insights or techniques. Again, the issue is not *either* God *or* modernity, but which in practice is the decisive authority. The superspiritual error is simply the opposite extreme. Just as Christians are flesh and blood as well as spirit, so the church of Christ is in the business of pews, parking lots, and planning committees as well as prayer and preaching.

Therefore the latest scientific study on parking lots has its place. But this is a far cry from the dictum of the church-growth gurus that, "The No. 1 rule of church growth is that a church will never get bigger than its parking lot."

Its parking lot? A dead giveaway for the suburbanness of church growth. And No. 1? Above growth in faith? Before growth in the Word and Spirit? God forbid. For the church of Christ, the latest sociological study never has more than a low-level place—even in a "freeway fellowship" culture, such as

California. What truly matters after the accumulated wisdom of modernity has been put to good use is that the *real* character of the church remains to be demonstrated, the *real* growth of the church remains to be seen. Otherwise we fall foul of the charge leveled by rock star Michael Been of the Call: "Everything that goes on in every major corporation goes on inside the church, except as a sideline the Church teaches religion."[4]

If Jesus Christ is true, the church is more than just another human institution. He alone is her head. He is her sole source and single goal. His grace uniquely is her effective principle. What moves her is not finally interchangeable with the dynamics of even the closest of sister institutions. When the best of modern insights and tools are in full swing, there should always be a remainder, an irreducible character that is more than the sum of all the human, the natural, and the organizational.

If Jesus Christ is the head of the church and hence the source and goal of its entire life, true growth is only possible in obedience to him. Conversely, if the church becomes detached from Jesus Christ and his word, it cannot truly grow however active and successful it may seem to be. However spectacular its development, it will prove disappointing in the end. However celebrated its progress, it will prove ultimately a falling away. The authentic movements in the church are those that are set in motion by God's decisive authority, especially the decisive authority of grace.

The notion of decisive authority and therefore of the remainder, the irreducible, the noninterchangeable, and the unquantifiable is fundamental to grace and to the church. The church of Christ is more than spiritual and theological, but never less. Only when first things are truly first, over even the best and most attractive of second things, will the church be free of idols, free to let God be God, free to be herself, and free to experience the growth that matters.

QUESTIONS FOR REFLECTION AND DISCUSSION

1. What do you think of the claim about a "standing or falling question" about church growth? (see page 35)

2. Why do you think the tools and insights of modernity are most dangerous when most effective? (see pages 37–38)

3. What about your local church would you put into the category of "a remainder, an irreducible character that is more than the sum of all the human, the natural, and the organizational"? (page 39)

2

<hr>

TWO MAIN ROOTS
OF THE CHALLENGE

THE SECOND REMINDER deals with a further problem modernity poses for the church-growth movement—that, because of the nature of its two main roots, modernity and its "new ground" are far deeper and more double-edged than many church-growth proponents realize.

Modernization and modernity remain widely misunderstood today. Some people, for example, turn them into a kind of "rich man's Marxism," a deterministic movement that will inevitably sweep the world with prosperity, progress, and democratic revolutions. Christians, however, tend to fall foul of a simpler misunderstanding. Many use the word modernity as if it were a fancy word for "change" or simply a matter of being "up to date." They therefore treat it as something simple and straightforward—as if one can understand it through monitoring the latest trends and statistics—and put it to use simply like a new fax machine or laser printer.

But modernity is much more than that. It refers to the character and system of the world produced by the forces of modernization and development—centered above all on the premise that the "bottom up" causation of human designs and products has now decisively replaced the "top down" causation of God and the supernatural.

Modernity is therefore not a fancy word for "change" and little of it can be understood merely by watching trends and keeping up with the latest technologies. To grasp modernity is a challenge—it requires an understanding of the whole, not simply just the parts. Ironically, when we wrestle with a tough-minded overview of modernity, it turns out to be far from modern.

Modernity's replacement of "top down" God-centered living with "bottom up" human-centered living represents a titanic revolution in human history and experience. We can trace its origins in two main ways. One way is to focus on human beings and the impact of their ideas. Thus, the road to modernity traces from the revolutionary changes in ideas to the way they have affected society throughout the centuries. This mode of analysis goes back at least to the seventeenth-century scientific revolution and follows the story through the eighteenth-century Enlightenment and the nineteenth-century romantic movement to the modernist and postmodernist movements in the twentieth century.

The rarer but equally important way to analyze modernity and face the challenge is to focus on society and social change. The line is traced in reverse as the story is followed from the revolutionary changes in society to the way they have affected ideas. This mode of analysis goes back to major structural and institutional developments—supremely those that resulted from the capitalist revolution in the fifteenth century, the technological and industrial revolution in the eighteenth century, and the communications revolution in the twentieth century.

This is not the place for a comprehensive analysis of the twin roots of modernity. What matters for our inquiry is this: The world of modernity that has been produced by such a combination of revolutionary forces must be taken with the utmost seriousness because its impact now pervades religion. Thus when the megachurch movement relies on the insights and tools of modernity for its "new ground," it does not rely on something that is neutral or entirely benevolent. At the very least, church-growth proponents should be aware of a gigantic paradox in the relationship between modernity and the Christian faith.

One way to express the paradox is to stress the point made earlier that modernity provides both the single greatest *opportunity* the church has ever faced and the single greatest *challenge* the church has ever faced. The opportunity exists because more people in more societies are more open to the gospel in the modern world than in any previous era in history. So modernity is to us what the Greek language and Roman roads were to the first-century disciples, and the printing press and sailing ships were to believers at the time of the Reformation.

And yet, after examining the impact of modernity on a sense of truth, transcendence, and tradition—and on a sense of the totality and integration of faith in every part of life—we can appreciate why modernity is also the single greatest challenge the church has ever faced. Such is the nature and extent of its damage to faith in many parts of the modernized world that it combines the subtlety of the challenge of gnosticism with the open menace of persecutions like those of Nero, Diocletian, and Mao Tse-tung. Some observers have labeled the lethal impact of modernity on religion as "iron cage," "gigantic steel hammer," "runaway juggernaut," and "acid rain of the spirit." Such descriptions are well merited.

Another way to express the paradox is that modernity simultaneously makes evangelism infinitely easier but discipleship infinitely harder. Ponder the fact that the twentieth century was heralded as "the Christian Century," summed up aptly at the beginning of the century in John R. Mott's slogan—"the evangelization of the world in this generation." Yet the century is ending, as Jacques Ellul says, in a situation closer to the saying of Jesus, "When the son of man comes, will he find faith on the earth?" The problem is not that Christians have disappeared, but that Christian faith has become so deformed. Under the influence of modernity, we modern Christians are literally capable of winning the world while losing our own souls.

Grappling with modernity's profound ambivalence toward faith is urgent but far from easy. For one thing, the theories and technologies of modernity are currently converging in a particularly potent manner. Take, for example, the "cheerful nihilism" of University of Virginia philosopher Richard Rorty, born of the logic of modern philosophical theory, and Madonna's film "Truth or Dare," born of the logic of modern technology. Some might wonder what the ivory towers of Mr. Jefferson's University have to do with the flickering screens of MTV. But the deep resemblances between the two are striking—the same dissolution of truth, the same disappearance of self-hood, the same crisis of the very meaning of meaning. Not so much a coincidence as a convergence, such dark overlaps between modern theory and technology mean that the sunnier neutral view of modernity is quite simply naive.

Further, grappling with modernity is urgent but difficult because most evangelicals have not faced up to its character, let alone its challenge. This stems largely from the way evangelicals think—when we do, for modernity has also transformed us into people who do not think. One reason for the distorted thinking is our predominant Anglo-Saxon heritage that tends to make us bits-and-pieces rather than big-picture thinkers. English-speaking evangelicals are marked by a consistent failure to take presuppositions seriously, and also have a corresponding bias toward data, statistics, and factoids—always the trees rather than the forest, always facts rather than the framework in which they make sense.

This old condition has grown acute today because it has been aggravated by the church-growth preference for empirical data over theory, which—as we shall see—is itself a central feature of modernity. The present critique, for example, was dismissed by one church-growth advocate as unhelpful because it is "ideological rather than fact-based." This reminds me of the revealing reply given by a Washington bureaucrat to a visiting scholar. In a discussion on environmental protection and the costs of human safety, the scholar suggested that "some people believe human life is priceless."

"We have no data on that," the government expert replied.

Another reason why American evangelicals have not faced up to modernity is that we are victims of a two-hundred-year condition of chronic anti-intellectualism. We are thus prone to a mindless pragmatism that never finally succeeds because it is never reflective about its agenda, let alone the wider horizon of events. Yet another reason is that the combined effect of these problems leaves evangelicals schizophrenic when thinking about technology. We characteristically focus on the message rather than the medium. Evangelicals therefore view technology's substance as malevolently evil (for example, television programming), but its forms as benignly innocent because they are neutral (for example, television technology).

Surely only a combination of such factors can explain evangelicalism's fateful shortsightedness in two directions: toward modernity and toward those parts of Scripture that, by application, are either critical of the premises of modernity or a needed antidote to its seductions. For example, what is the theological meaning of God's anger at King David for succumbing to the devil's temptation to rely on numbers? (1 Chronicles 21, 27) Why was Uzzah killed and David judged for the wrong way the ark of God was taken to Jerusalem? (2 Samuel 6:7) Why was Asa condemned because he "resorted to physicians" rather than seeking guidance of the LORD? (2 Chronicles 16:12) Why was Israel judged in the reign of Hezekiah for fortifying their walls, stockpiling their weapons, and harnessing the water resources, "but you did not look to the One who made it"? (Isaiah 22:11)

Anyone who ponders such passages can only wonder at the contrast between the enduring realism of Scripture and our dismaying gullibility in the face of modernity.

QUESTIONS FOR REFLECTION AND DISCUSSION

1. Describe from your own experience how "modernity," as I use the term, has a day-to-day impact on your life. What do you think are the advantages and disadvantages of modernity as far as your Christian discipleship is concerned? (see pages 43–44)

2. What aspects of our modern discipleship and church life would appear most strange or perhaps even unbiblical to a Christian from the early church or from the time of the Reformation?

3. Why you think God severely judged David for counting the people of Israel? (see page 45)

3

THREE MAIN DANGERS
OF MODERNITY

THE THIRD REMINDER deals with yet another way modernity poses
problems for the church-growth movement—through its direct
damage to faith. Here at last, one might expect, there would be
a realistic understanding of modernity. But in fact most Christian
believers have not faced up to modernity's fundamental damage
to faith for several reasons.

One reason it is easy to overlook modernity's damage to religion is that the overall consequences of modernization are so
positive. Which of us, for example, would choose to go back to
previous generations if we considered the blessings of health
alone, not to speak of the advantages of travel and communication?

Another reason many overlook the damage done by modernity is that it was previously stated and overstated by open ene-
mies of the faith who had an obvious ax to grind. In the great
heyday of secularism, for example, modernity was cited with an
almost mantra-like authority, so that everything modern was
automatically taken as "progressive" and "irreversible" while
everything religious was reactionary and fated to disappear. Such
views are now acknowledged to be both wrong and biased. Many
Christians, in turn, are so relieved that modernity is not as bad as
they thought that they have thrown out an estimate of its real
damage along with the exaggerated accounts.

47

Once the exaggerations have been removed, however, modernity's real damage must be faced. For certain lethal trends are at work in the principles and processes of modernity. Once again, a comprehensive account would take us a long way from our task. But there is broad agreement on the three main trends reckoned to be the culprits.

Stated briefly, the three damaging trends are *secularization*, *privatization*, and *pluralization*. Through secularization, modernity removes successive sectors of modern society from the decisive influence of religious ideas and institutions. Through privatization, modernity produces a cleavage between the private and public sectors of life—the private sector commonly being the only place where religion is free to flourish. Through pluralization, modernity multiplies the number of options people have in the private sphere at all levels—including that of faiths, worldviews, and ideologies. The result of this pluralization is a greater sense of relativism, subjectivism, uncertainty, and anxiety surrounding religion in the modern world.

Unquestionably the component that bears directly on the church-growth movement is what Max Weber called "rationalization." This is the first of the two underlying dynamics of secularization (the other is differentiation). Rationalization has meant that religious ideas are less meaningful and religious institutions are more marginal because of modernity's advance. More and more of what was formerly left to God, human initiative, or the processes of nature is now classified, calculated, and controlled by the systematic application of reason and technique. What counts in the rationalized world is efficiency, predictability, quantifiability, productivity, the substitution of technology for the human, and—from first to last—control over uncertainty.

For religion, the result of rationalization is what Weber also called "disenchantment" (and C. S. Lewis called "a new enchantment"). All the "magic and mystery" of life is reduced and removed—not so much unwanted as unnecessary. No one in the process is necessarily hostile to religion. Rather, as technique and the "figure it out" rationality spread further and further, the decisiveness of faith is rendered more and more irrelevant. As social scientist Philip Rieff sums it up, "What characterizes modernity, I think, is just this idea that men need not submit to any power—higher or lower—other than their own."[1]

Whether said with defiance by the few or left unsaid but practiced by the many, religion that is irrelevant in practice becomes practically irrelevant. There is no need for God, even in his church.

Put differently, and in distinct contrast to the widespread conservative fallacy of the eighties, the sharpest challenge of modernity is not secularism, but secularization. Secularism is a philosophy; secularization is a process. Whereas the philosophy is obviously hostile and touches only a few, the process is largely invisible and touches many. Being openly hostile, secularism rarely deceives Christians. Being much more subtle, secularization often deceives Christians before they are aware of it, including those in the church-growth movement. How else can one explain the comment of a Japanese businessman to a visiting Australian? "Whenever I meet a Buddhist leader, I meet a holy man. Whenever I meet a Christian leader, I meet a manager."

The two most easily recognizable hallmarks of secularization in America are the exaltation of numbers and of technique. Both are prominent in the megachurch movement at a popular level. In its fascination with statistics and data at the expense of truth, this movement is characteristically modern.

Some people argue that the emphasis on quantifiable measures—on counting—is the central characteristic of a rationalized society. Thus the United States has government by polling, television programming by ratings, sports commentary by statistics, education by grade-point averages, and academic tenure by the number of publications. In such a world of number crunchers, bean counters, and computer analysts, the growth of churches as a measurable, "fact-based" business enterprise is utterly natural.

One obvious problem with this mentality is that quantity does not measure quality. Numbers—or what the Southern Baptists call "nickels and noses"—have little to do with truth, excellence, or character. As one sociologist says, "Big Mac," even with billions and billions of hamburgers served, need not mean "Good Mac." But what is misleading even at the trivial level of fast food becomes dangerous as one moves through sports prowess, educational attainment, and presidential character to spiritual depth. For church growth viewed in measurable terms, such as numbers, is trivial compared with growth in less measurable but more important terms, such as faith, character, and godliness. Having growth in terms of numbers, of course, does not rule out the more important spiritual growth. But it does not necessarily include this type of growth either.

Behind this problem lie other problems. Christians would do well to ponder the aversion to a counting and calculating mentality that takes numbers too far. This is so evident in both the Scriptures and many traditional societies. For a start, traditional people believed that the calculating mentality was closely linked to the deadly sin of avarice. Avarice, in this view, is not the love of possessions so much as the love of possessing. Counting is therefore the chief pleasure of the miser and money is most pleasurable counting of all. Thus people and things are annihilated in the process of counting. They lose their true purpose and joy and become mere status symbols—just as church membership statistics become hollow symbols when used to advertise pastors, churches, and methodologies rather than representing real people with their flesh and blood realities.

In addition, traditional people eschewed the counting and calculating mentality because it was linked to a desire for control. The progression is plain: What was classified could be counted, what was counted could be calculated, and what was calculated could be controlled. Thus one explanation for the Old Testament prohibition on numbering the people was that the census stood for the royal power to regiment the people to its own purposes even while pretending to serve God's. Counting was therefore critical to the rising power of royal ideology in subtle but profound opposition to the sovereignty and role of God. It was the fatal step away from David's radical, unsupported trust in

God toward the vast standing army of Solomon, under which a call to arms became an exercise in royal power rather than what it was earlier: a response to the mobilization of God's Spirit.

Are there not similar dangers when a numbers-hungry church mimics the high-control calculus of modern commercial enterprises? "Totally planned, professionally orchestrated, single-purpose environments" may be as "effective" for evangelism in megachurches as they are for selling in megamalls. But when everything is controlled, from first impressions in the parking lot to the wardrobe colors and stage movements of the platform party, who controls the church and who controls the controllers? Something of the mysterious and lovable but unwashed reality of the real-life bride of Christ is lost. Something of the impossible-to-predict, category-shattering sovereignty and grace of God is walled off.

Lastly, the Scriptures and traditional societies showed an aversion to the calculating mentality because it was closely linked to human self-reliance and therefore to the risk of presumption before God. The biblical prohibition against numbering the people was a safeguard against human presumption that paralleled similar customs in many traditional societies. Algerian *fellahs*, or peasants, for example, traditionally refuse to measure their seedcorn and only measure their harvest cautiously "so as not to presume on God's generosity."[7] Zealous church-growth salespeople, evangelists who trumpet the calculus of their cost-per-convert successes, and Christian politicians who forever invoke the 20 to 30 million evangelicals purportedly ready to "pray and vote" for their watershed cause would all do well to reflect on this humility and the reasons behind it.

A telltale preoccupation with technique also prominent in the church-growth movement is linked to secularization. Life is viewed as a set of problems, each set having a rational solution, an identifiable expert, and therefore a practical mechanism to effect it. Take the example of *Leadership Journal*, the best-known evangelical magazine for pastors and church life, one that deals with the problems of leadership in the churches. A recent analysis showed that over the course of time the magazine had examined almost every conceivable church problem in its pages. Yet, believe it or not, less than one percent of the articles had any reference to Scripture at all, or any serious theological component.[3] It was not surprising when *Leadership*'s analysis of the church-growth movement on its twenty-first birthday was purely statistical, not theological. In the form of the imperialistic genius of managerial and therapeutic insights, galloping secularization left theology in the dust.

Or take the example of the changing profiles of the pastor. Needless to say, distortions of the ministry are not new. In 1886, *Nation* magazine reported: "Indeed, so far has the church caught the spirit of the age, so far has it become a business enterprise, that the chief test of ministerial success is now the ability to 'build up' a church. Executive, managerial abilities are now more in demand than those which used to be considered the highest in a clergyman."[4]

A century later, the distortions have deepened and grown characteristically modern. Thus in a massive study in 1934, pastors were said to have five distinct roles—teacher, preacher, pastor, leader, and administrator.[5] These roles are notable for being few in number and biblical in content. But in another huge study in 1980, involving forty-seven denominations, evidence showed that the pastor's profile both expanded and grew more secular. Pastors were expected to be open, affirming, able to foster relationships, experienced in facilitating discussion, and so on. The new premium was on skills in interpersonal relationships and conflict management. Biblical and spiritual criteria of ministry were notably optional.

Yet another study in 1986 showed that the differences in expectations between liberals and evangelicals had almost disappeared, that secular expectations grew while the spiritual shrunk, and that the profile was largely dominated by two sets of considerations—those therapeutic and managerial.[6]

Anyone who doubts this shift has only to look at church-growth literature and check for such chapters as "Portrait of the effective pastor." In one such best-seller, theology and theological references are kept to a minimum—little more than a cursory reference to the pastor's "personal calling" and to "God's vision for the church." The bulk of the chapter is taken up with such themes as delegating, confidence, interaction, decision making, visibility, practicality, accountability, and discernment—the profile of the thoroughly modern pastor as CEO.

Unquestionably the discussion is admirable. But unquestionably too the discussion is only of "the interchangeable." There is nothing about the "irreducible," the "remainder," and the otherwise inexplicable. Thus the leadership qualities could apply in a hundred other organizations—after all, they once did, and were simply borrowed. Worse still, the disadvantage of the CEO-Pastor, as increasing numbers of them are discovering, is that those who live like CEOs are fired like CEOs—and spiritual considerations have as little to do with the ending as with the beginning and the middle. Small wonder that one eminent Christian leader returned home from a church-growth conference puzzled. There had been "literally no theology," he said. "In fact, there had been no serious reference to God at all."

QUESTIONS FOR REFLECTION AND DISCUSSION

1. When you think of the pastors and Christian leaders that you know, are they closer to "holy men" or "managers"? (see page 49)

2. If numbers, counting, and calculation have a built-in secularizing tendency, what place do they have in your church experience?

3. When you think over your experience in church life and witnessing, is the place of technique balanced by such considerations as truth, character, and knowing God? Or is technique becoming the driving preoccupation?

FOUR MAIN STEPS
IN COMPROMISE

THE FOURTH REMINDER deals with the dynamics of compromise with the world. Christian history is a two-thousand-year conversation between the church and the world. As Christians we are called to be in the world, but not of it. Throughout the centuries Christians have lived out this tension in many ways. Some, at the one extreme, have been neither of the world nor in it, and therefore have been isolated. Others, at the other extreme, have been both in the world and of it, and therefore have been compromised.

Doubtless, few on either side would disagree with the ideals of the other, though cultural conservatives would stress the ideal of resistance to the world and cultural liberals would stress relevance in it. At the same time, almost no one would dispute that the biblical challenge is to be balanced. Everyone, however extreme in reality, would consider his or her own position the perfect model of balance. Beyond question, too, evangelicals have traditionally been toward the conservative pole, stressing cognitive defiance; whereas liberals have been on the progressive side, emphasizing cognitive bargaining with the cultured despisers of the gospel.

But today we are confronted with a staggering change in the dynamism of this age-old dialogue. At the high noon of modernity, the influence of the world has become so powerful, pervasive, and appealing that the traditional stance of cognitive defiance has become rare and almost unthinkable.

For example, it is commonly said of contemporary evangelicals that we are "of" the world while still not "in it"—because of our uncritical use of such everyday things as VCRs. People who, a generation ago, would have considered it "worldly" to go to the cinema now view films in their own homes that would have been unthinkable to much of the "world" before. Mind you, they still may not go to the cinema, but in almost everything else they have changed. Both in and of the world, many evangelicals are now out-doing liberals as the enthusiastic religious modernizers—and compromisers—of today.

Compromise is compromise regardless of when, how, or why it happens—though certainly there are qualifications to it. Thus Christian compromise with the world is usually unconscious, and not deliberate. It can be a matter of lifestyle as easily as belief. And, mercifully, few people go the whole way. Nonetheless, the Christian must recognize and counter the four distinct steps involved in compromise with the thinking or behavior of the world.

The first and crucial step toward compromise is that of *assumption*. Nothing may be further from a believer's mind than compromise, but like the Chinese journey of a thousand miles, the road to compromise begins in a small way. Some aspect of modern life or thought is entertained not only as significant, and therefore worth acknowledging, but as superior to what Christians now know or do, and therefore worth assuming as true.

The second step toward compromise is *abandonment*. Everything that does not fit in with the new assumption (made in step one) is either discounted or cut out. What is involved in this step is not just a matter of altering tactics but of altering truth itself. Something modern is assumed to be true and proper. Therefore everything that is no longer assertable in the face of it must go.

The third step toward compromise is that of *adaptation*. Something new is assumed, something old is abandoned, and everything else is adapted. In other words, what remains of traditional beliefs and practices is altered to fit in with the new assumption. It is translated into the language and expectations of the new assumption, which becomes the controlling assumption.

The fourth step toward compromise is *assimilation*. This is the logical culmination of the first three. Something modern is assumed (step one). As a consequence, something traditional is abandoned (step two), and everything else is adapted (step three). At the end of the line, Christian assumptions are absorbed by the modern ones. The gospel has been assimilated to the shape of culture, often without a remainder.

General examples of compromise are not usually controversial or hard to see, especially from the past. For example, when the church's compromise was with civil religion, the gospel was domesticated; when it was with existentialism, the gospel was lobotomized historically; when it was with logical positivism, the gospel was pruned; when it was with process theology, the gospel lost its absolutes; when it was with situation ethics, the gospel was sentimentalized, and so on.

At the same time, individual examples of compromise from the past are easy to see, especially those by prominent liberals. It was said of Adolf Harnack, for example, that "the Christ Harnack sees. . . is only the reflection of a Liberal Protestant face seen at the bottom of a deep well."[1] Or we may remember Rudolf Bultmann's celebrated argument that modern people cannot use electric light and radio or call upon medicine in the case of illness and at the same time believe in the New Testament world of spirits and miracles. Without realizing it, Bultmann illustrates the shift from a description that is proper ("the scientific worldview has tended to increase secularity") to a judgment that does not necessarily follow ("the scientific worldview makes the New Testament worldview incredible"). In the process he compromised.

Perhaps the most blatant example of this perverse bias toward compromise was the World Council of Churches' dictum in 1966, "The world must set the agenda for the Church." Three decades later, it is hard to believe that such an advance warning of preemptive capitulation could have been trumpeted as a lofty and self-evident principle. But it is also worth checking to see whether there are similar inanities in the church-growth movement today.

Take, for example, the current church-growth infatuation with marketing the church. It echoes Bruce Barton's 1920s' bestseller, *The Man Nobody Knows*, which portrayed Jesus as "the founder of modern business" and his parables as "the most powerful advertisements of all time." Apparently, Jesus' saying "I must be about my Father's business" was taken with a literalistic seriousness worthy of a Muslim fundamentalist.

It still is. Consider the progression in the following sentences from church-growth treatment of the subject: "The Church is a business."/"Marketing is essential for a business to operate successfully."/"The Bible is one of the world's great marketing texts."/"However, the point is indisputable: the Bible does not warn against the evils of marketing."/"So it behooves us not to spend time bickering about techniques and processes."/"Think of your church not as a religious meeting place, but as a service agency—an entity that exists to satisfy people's needs."/"The marketing plan is the Bible of the marketing game; everything that happens in the life of the product occurs because the plan wills it."

This string of truths, half-truths, quarter-truths, and flat-out errors comes to a climax in a statement that is utterly wrong and deadly, yet to much of the church-growth movement nothing short of canonical: "It is also critical that we keep in mind a fundamental principle of Christian communication: the audience, not the message, is sovereign."

Is it correct that the "sovereign audience" is "a fundamental principle of Christian communication"? This is a dangerously distorted half-truth and a recycling of the error of classical lib-

eralism. This approach to the affluent consumers of the twentieth century carries the same seeds of compromise as Friedrich
Schleiermacher's approach to the cultured despisers of the gospel
in the eighteenth century.

Like the Bereans in the New Testament, we have to examine
such statements for ourselves and make our own biblical assessment. But while many people still appear moonstruck by the
recent discovery of the sovereign audience, it is worth pondering
a *New Yorker* lament about what is lost in the brave, new "audience-driven" preaching of the day: "The preacher, instead of
looking out upon the world, looks out upon public opinion, trying to find out what the public would like to hear. Then he tries
his best to duplicate that, and bring his finished product into a
marketplace in which others are trying to do the same. The public, turning to our culture to find out about the world, discovers
there is nothing but its own reflection. The unexamined world,
meanwhile, drifts blindly into the future."[2]

QUESTIONS FOR REFLECTION AND DISCUSSION

1. List the four stages of compromise and ask yourself whether you see any examples of it, even unwitting ones, in your current Christian thinking and practice.

2. Where is the half-truth and where is the dangerous error in the church-growth principle: "the audience, not the message, is sovereign"? (see page 58)

3. Is such thinking different in principle or only in degree from the classical liberal strategy of reaching "the cultured despisers of the gospel"? (see pages 58–59)

5

FIVE MAIN IRONIES

THE FIFTH REMINDER deals with the unintended consequences of Christians engaging uncritically with modernity. Irony, ironically, is a profoundly biblical theme that does not figure strongly in the thinking of most Christians. Yet no other religion rivals the Christian faith in providing such a foundation for a strong view of irony. Because human unbelief is essentially a matter of the "truth held in unrighteousness," Christians can always count on the fact that the "truth will come out" regardless of the denials of unbelief, that the consequences of human action will always be other than we intended, and that reality will always have the last laugh. Irony, in short, is not merely a subject for writers or cultural commentators; it is a key part of the Christian understanding of life.

It takes a developed sense of irony to appreciate the present position of Protestant evangelicalism in America. This is significant for our discussion because evangelicalism is the source and chief exponent of the church-growth movement. These ironies are stated briefly, without comment.

First, Protestants today need the most protesting and reforming. Second, evangelicals and fundamentalists have become the most worldly tradition in the church. Third, conservatives are becoming the most progressive. Fourth, Christians in many cases are the prime agents of their own secularization. Fifth, through its uncritical engagement with modernity, the church is becoming its own most effective gravedigger.

I first appreciated the momentousness of these ironies when one of Europe's leading sociologists turned to me at the end of a seminar at Oxford University in the mid-seventies and asked:

"By the end of the 1970s, who will be the worldliest Christians in America?" Somewhat uncertain what he was after, I let him answer his own question.

"It'll be the fundamentalists," he said.

At the time, more than a decade before the scandals of televangelism, that was a startling claim. Fundamentalism, after all, prided itself on being world-denying by definition. Today, however, it has become world-affirming in a worldlier and more compromising way than most contemporary movements in liberalism.

Mention of the liberal camp only deepens the irony. If fundamentalists as modernity's former misfits have become its most ardent missionaries, liberals, who once pursued modernity's cultural despisers to the point of "addictive accommodationism" appear somewhat sobered. Liberalism, far more than evangelicalism, is marked today by its "recovery movements" that delve back into tradition. Liberals, not evangelicals, are in the forefront of the writing of serious new systematic theologies.

For the church-growth movement, what matters are the breeding grounds in which such ironies and unintended consequences multiply. Two are paramount. The first breeding ground is the more traditional one: the uncritical espousal of the ideal of "relevance" and its companion church-growth slogans, "seeker-friendly," "audience-driven," and "full-service churches."

As stated earlier, relevance is a prerequisite for communication. Without it, there is no communication, only a one-sided sending of messages addressed to no one, nowhere. But having said that, it must also be said that relevance is a more complex, troublesome, and seductive matter than its advocates acknowledge.

For a start, relevance is a question-begging concept when invoked by itself. And when absolutized, relevance becomes lethal to truth. Properly speaking, relevance assumes and requires the answer to such questions as: Relevance for what? Relevant to whom? If these questions are left unasked, a constant appeal to relevance becomes a way of riding roughshod over truth and corralling opinion coercively. People are thinking or doing something simply "because it is relevant" without knowing why. But truth, in fact, gives relevance to "relevance," just as "relevance" becomes irrelevance if it is not related to truth. Without truth, relevance is meaningless and dangerous.

In addition, relevance has a false allure that masks both its built-in transience and its catch-22 demand. Dean Inge captured the transience in his celebrated line "He who marries the spirit of the age soon becomes a widower." But it was Simone Weil who highlighted the catch-22: "To be always relevant, you have to say things which are eternal."

Modernity makes this problem worse. Compounded by the conforming tendency of a mass society, relevance without truth encourages what Nietzsche called the "herd" mentality and Kierkegaard "the age of the crowd." Further compounded by accelerating change, which itself is compounded by the fashion-driven dictates of consumerism, relevance becomes overheated and vaporizes into trendiness. The result, Nietzsche warns, is feverishness. "Under the aspect of eternity" (*sub specie aeternitatis*) becomes "under the aspect of fifteen minutes." Instead of "the contentment of a tree in its roots, the happiness of knowing that one is not wholly accidental and arbitrary but grown out of a past as its heir, flower, and fruit," feverishness is the condition of an institution that has ceased to be faithful to its origins. It is then caught up in "a restless, cosmopolitan hunting after new and ever newer things."[1]

The pursuit of relevance thus becomes a prime source of superficiality, anxiety, and burn-out. ("Hell," it has been said, "will be full of newspapers with a fresh edition every thirty seconds, so that no one will ever feel caught up.") In its competitive—read "marketed"—form, relevance becomes "trendier than thou" and eventually becomes the fast road toward irrelevance. Revealingly, when "Saturday Night Live" becomes a church's seeker-friendly "Sunday Morning Live" and "The Best Show in Town," the typical church staff question after worship becomes "How did it go?"

For many evangelicals, relevance as the road to irrelevance is still tomorrow's problem rather than today's. But the fate of liberalism should give evangelicals occasion to pause. Evangelicals would do well to ponder the enigma of relevance more deeply. One lesson from the "road to Rome" or the "Canterbury trail" is the advantage of "irrelevance" being transcultural and transhistorical. Precisely because the gospel carries the oxygen of eternity, it allows modern people to catch their breath as they pant breathlessly toward their temporal goals. Precisely because the church crosses cultures and generations, G. K. Chesterton could even boast that "The Catholic Church is the only thing which saves a man from being the degraded child of his own age."[2] There is thus an irrelevance to the pursuit of relevance as well as a relevance to the practice of irrelevance.

Is this too subtle for our evangelical pragmatists? If so, their pragmatism is most impractical. Henri Nouwen makes an unmistakably simple counterpoint to church-growth teaching: "I am deeply convinced that the Christian leader of the future is called to be completely irrelevant. . . . That is the way Jesus came to reveal God's love."[3]

The second and more modern breeding ground for irony is the church-growth movement's uncritical elevation of modern notions of "need." The megachurches' entire law, as one proponent puts it, is summed up in their two great commandments: "Find a need and meet it, find a hurt and heal it."

At first sight, a ministry based on meeting needs is surely unobjectionable. After all, its ultimate sanction is the saying of Jesus: "It is not the healthy who need a doctor, but the sick. I have not come to call the righteous, but sinners to repentance" (Luke 5:31–32). Need is thus the proper first step toward both true faith and prayer. As George Macdonald wrote, "Every need of God. . . is a seeking of God, is a begging for himself, is profoundest prayer, and the root and inspirer of all other prayer."[4]

Properly understood, need is not the first step toward faith because searchers believe in God because of needs. Rather, searchers become searchers because they come to disbelieve what they once believed because of needs that their previous faith could not answer. They are then open to discovering the truth of the good news of Jesus Christ.

Yet people who use the modern need-meeting approach overlook certain things. First, this approach has no matching emphasis in truth, and leaves the church carelessly vulnerable to intellectual dismissal. The heirs of Ludwig Feuerbach and Sigmund Freud, for instance, attack the church by charging that "the fundamental dogmas of Christianity are fulfilled wishes of the heart"—which is in fact a fair description of much modern evangelical believing.

Second, meeting needs does not always satisfy needs; it often stokes further ones and raises the pressure of eventual disillusionment. As Immanuel Kant said to a Russian historian Karamzin, "Give a man everything he desires and yet at this very moment he will feel that everything is not everything." The outcome is a massive pandering to the pathology of a consumerist age.

Third, and even more importantly, modernity has expanded and corrupted the very notion of need by creating a "need on command" society. Needs, consumerism, and professionalism are the three pillars of our modern service society. To be need-less is to be less than human. As sociologist Tony Walters points out, modern consumer society is built on a grand reversal of the Beatles' song: "All you love is need."

A generation ago, one analyst writes, "*problems* existed only in mathematics or chess; *solutions* were saline or legal, and *need* was mainly a verb. The expressions 'I have a problem,' or 'I have a need' both sounded silly." Today, however, need—used as a noun—has become socially respectable and even fashionable.

"To be ignorant or unconvinced of one's own needs," says Ivan Illich, "has become the unforgivable anti-social act."[5] And unlike natural resources, such as land, needs have no natural limits. There is no end to the needs and need-meeting services that can be manufactured and distributed.

Strikingly, the new status of "need" has simultaneously debased true needs and elevated a new generation of experts—because of their authority to describe and prescribe. Need, subject to consumer fashion, becomes shallow, plastic, and manipulable. Needs induced by advertising slogans are often merely wants; as such, they become commodities that are purchased on command through expert prescription. Thus from books to newspapers to movies to television to videos, American culture is becoming a vast, lucrative exercise in need-meeting and appetite satisfaction on a mass scale. Epitomized by the incessant drive to produce "blockbusters," the result is a descent into vulgarity and adolescence that stands as a warning to any who make Need primary and find meeting Need easy.

As one Christian publisher cautions, "Do books which speak to and resolve basic human personal needs. Puff the benefits and chase celebrities. . . Promise them the stars, the sun, and the moon, and you will gain the world. It's as easy as that. It's no secret. *But watch the soul!*"[6]

For Christians, the modern use of need creates two still deeper problems. One is that it debases the Bible's revolutionary attitude to need and becomes a way of adjusting the needy to the status quo. A need met this way is a needy person quieted and a potential disciple co-opted.

In the Scripture, by contrast, cries of pain and grief are an important step toward repudiating the numbing wrongness of the status quo. "Never soul was set free," George Macdonald writes, "without being made to feel its slavery."[7] First, cries of pain and grief have a different audience than modern notions of need. In rising to God, cries of pain and grief turn decisively from all no-gods and non-listeners. Second, they have a different content than modern notions of need. The Hebrew notion of crying out is more a complaint and a deliberate legal plea than a lament. Third, they have a different purpose than modern notions of need. In the Scripture, meeting the need is only the prelude to meeting God and thus to a life of worship and radical freedom that includes a dismantling of the old orders of injustice through the new realities of God's rule.

Will the church-growth and megachurch movement prove a worthy successor of earlier movements of evangelical revival in proving socially revolutionary as it responds to human needs? First signs are not encouraging.

The other problem with the modern use of need is that, endlessly engineered and marketed, an obsession with need results in consumer indifference to *specific, genuine, real* needs. People skilled in learning to need the needs that the professional elites identify become deaf to their own true needs—their needs as God, not the world, defines them.

In short, the exaggerated half-truth about the church's "needing to meet needs" once again breeds unintended consequences. Just as church-growth's modern passion for "relevance" will become its road to irrelevance, so its modern passion for "felt needs" will turn the church into an echo chamber of fashionable needs that drown out the one voice that addresses real human need below all felt needs. After all, if true needs are a first step toward faith and prayer, false needs are the opposite. As George Macdonald observed again, "that need which is no need, is a demon sucking at the spring of your life."[10]

Questions for Reflection and Discussion

1. What place in your faith do you give to the ironies and un-intended consequences of life that are a result of sin and a fallen world? What does this mean for our well-intentioned endeavors? (see page 61)

2. What do you see as the pros and cons of the pursuit of relevance? (see pages 62–64)

3. Where do you see the gospel of the New Testament distorted by modern assumptions and expectations about "need"? (see pages 64–67)

6

SIX MAIN CARRIERS OF MODERNITY

THE SIXTH REMINDER deals with the people who are likely to become the source of the church's problem, because of church growth's uncritical engagement with modernity.

The term "carrier" is often used of modernization, borrowed from the medical field to express the development equivalent of a carrier of disease. Usually the reference is to impersonal, structural forces—such as urbanization, the spread of the market economy, bureaucratization, and so on. But it is useful to remember that modernity is also "carried" by certain character types—in other words, by people whose jobs and skills are the epitome of different parts of the modernization process.

There are six main carriers, or character types, of modernity. One or two others might be added. But not only are they close to the essence of modernity; they are very close to some of us, a recognition that can be disturbing.

First is the *pundit*, the one for whom "everything can be known, everything can be pronounced on," centered professionally on the importance of information.

Second is the *engineer*, the one for whom "everything can be designed, everything can be produced," centered professionally on production. (You want to market a perfume, land a man on the moon, plant a new church? The engineer will figure it out.)

Third is the *marketer*, the one for whom "everything can be positioned, everything can be sold," centered professionally on consumer satisfaction.

Fourth is the *consultant*, the one for whom "everything can be better organized, everything can be better delivered," centered professionally on management.

Fifth is the *therapist*, the one for whom "everything can be gotten in touch with, everything can be adjusted or healed," centered professionally on healing.

Sixth is the *impresario*, the one for whom "everything can be conveyed to advantage through the presentation of images regardless of any reality," centered professionally on public relations and "impression management."

Doubtless several of these carriers come close to many of us and all of them merit deeper discussion. I will expand only on the pundit because of its importance in the proliferation of church-growth gurus and management consultants.

Modernity breeds pundits; indeed it turns modern society into a punditocracy based on the ruling assumption that everything can be known, everything can be pronounced upon. Many factors contribute to the pundit's appeal: the arrival of the knowledge society, the rising status of information and data (and the person whom novelist Robert Musil calls "a dipsomaniac whose tipple is facts"), the triumph of the New Class, the importance of "ideas brokers" and the "culture wars" (America now has more than a thousand think tanks), the rise of professional, credentialed experts, and the introduction of an entertainment dynamic in thinking (so that we now have gurus-in-residence and intellectual celebrities with a passion to perform). Two other elements that favor the pundit are the rise of short-attention discourse (promoted by television's incredible shrinking sound bite) and the hunger for meaning and belonging with its attendant growth of prophecy and future-hype.

Put all these factors together and the rise of the pundit becomes natural, and even necessary. Nor does it take much thought to see its influence. Take the example of the role of pundits on such political talk shows as "Crossfire," "The Capital

Gang," and "The McLaughlin Group." The features of such shows are well known: the trivializing of issues, the sound-bite reasoning, the contrived aggression, the locker room machoism, the off-camera celebrity pimping for corporations, and the considerable hypocrisy—the same people who expect to be taken seriously when they write in newspapers do not expect to be taken seriously when they josh around on the talk shows. Yet their pundit power to set agendas is enormous. Informed opinion in America has become the replay of yesterday's talk show.

Needless to say, Christian pundits are somewhat different in both subject matter and style. But the differences are less than one should expect and not as important as the less obvious similarities. Two problems commonly develop. First, overreliance on pundits—or on any of the other carriers—leads Christians toward *dependency on professionalism and expertise.* While Christian ministry is the prototype of the profession, and such traditional professions as law and medicine were openly altruistic as a reflection of their origin, modern professionalism has a different goal and a different outcome.

Professionalism embodies the power to prescribe. Today it is the key to determining need, defining clients, delivering solutions, and deepening dependency— whether in healing identity, rebuilding inner cities, dispensing public opinion, or planting churches among baby boomers.

The result, however, is not necessarily greater freedom and responsibility for ordinary people, because the dominance of the expert means the dependency of the client. All that has changed is the type of authority. Traditional authorities, such as the clergy, have been replaced by modern authorities—in this case, denominational leaders by church-growth experts. The outcome is what Christopher Lasch calls "paternalism without a father" and Ivan Illich "the age of disabling professions."[1] The suggestion is that "The expert knows best," so "we can do better." But the "ministry of *all* believers" recedes once again. Even the dream of the "self-help" movement becomes a radical chic illusion that disguises the gold rush of experts in its wake. In most cases, all that has changed is the type of clergy. The old priesthood is dead! Long live the new power-pastors and pundit-priests!

Second, overreliance on pundits leads Christians toward *disregard for the specifically Christian content of the expertise*. In the case of the Christian pundit, for example, a dazzling grasp of modern data and information often obscures a striking blind spot—his or her lack of attention to theological discernment or to matters of wisdom, responsibility, and character, which in Scripture far outweigh the importance of information.

More seriously still, uncritical adulation of the Christian pundit runs the risk of opening the doors to modern varieties of false prophets. Jeremiah, you will remember, distinguished the false from the true with his searching question: "But which of them has stood in the council of the LORD to see or to hear his word?" (Jeremiah 23:18) I read Jeremiah's question and can only say, "Have I? Have we?" That divine source alone divides true Christian speaking from false. Without it, all prophecy is false, all punditry shallow—the mere chatter of recycled opinions and retailed personal fancies.

QUESTIONS FOR REFLECTION AND DISCUSSION

1. Which of the six "carriers" of modernity have you seen most active and appreciated (and therefore potentially dangerous) in your church and Christian experience?

2. Who are your main "pundits" in both the secular world and the Christian world? What steps do you take to check them discerningly and stop yourself from growing too dependent on their expertise?

3. Do you know of widely accepted Christian experts whose opinions and findings are taken as "gospel" when really they are only a Christian rehash of conventional secular wisdom?

SEVEN MAIN TIPS
FOR DISCERNMENT

THE SEVENTH REMINDER is a checklist of considerations to help sharpen discernment when using modern insights and tools. As stressed before, the purpose is to ensure that we are still dining with long enough spoons, that our idol-sounding hammers are in good trim, and that our ears are still tuned to the sound of hollowness.

First, ask what the emperor is wearing today. Like many movements in their expansion phase, the church-growth movement needs checking for claims and statements that have outrun reality. The only thing worse than a gullible public is a cocky emperor whose self-importance and passion for novelty blinds him to his own nakedness.

Against this danger, we need to work hard to preserve the clear sight and unspoiled forthrightness of the small boy who is ever unimpressed by the latest designer fashions. The way to do this is to remember that all critique, however sophisticated or elementary, is a matter of asking three simple questions: What is being said? Is it true? What should be done?

It obviously does not take a philosopher or textual critic to understand these three questions. But when employed, they cut through the tangles and pomposities of inflated claims like a scythe.

It would be easy to critique the "vogue for the vague" in new self-descriptions spawned by the megachurch movement (one superchurch in Houston calls itself "A Fellowship of Excitement"). But at a more serious level, take the example of the style of speaking and writing that is common in the movement, especially when it relies heavily on demographic studies and futurism. Much of it is a mind-numbing cataract of words that is part statistical barrage and part rhetorical massage. Speeches, books, and workshops foam and sparkle with a torrent of such terms as crisis, challenge, change, change agent, new paradigm, wake-up call, dynamism, opportunity, new dimensions, difference maker, devising strategies, reinventing organizations, emergent, innovative, revolutionary, and entrepreneurial.

Like the words themselves, the listener is easily carried away. They flow over us like a powerful shower, leaving our minds alternately tingling with excitement or shivering with apprehension, but questionless either way. Too often, we never get around to asking, What is being said? And more importantly, Is it true? And what should be done?

Marketing language is already the source of an eerie hollowness throughout American society. But as business columnist Robert Samuelson warns, we must also beware the "numskull factor" in managerial writing. "Our corporate elites are awash in empty jargon that masquerades as serious thought."[1] The same shallowness must be resisted in church-growth language, regardless of its spiritual component. Silly claims supercharged in solemn words are still just silly claims. The pink flesh may be imperial but it is still undressed.

Second, note whose the bottom line is. Like every human idea and institution east of Eden, the church-growth movement is a matter of both ideas that serve ideals and ideas that serve interests. Thus when dealing with a movement that openly insists on viewing religion in marketing terms, and ceaselessly cites "the bottom line" as if it were a sacred text, we must ask not only "What is the bottom line?" but "*Whose* is the bottom line?" Behind the service is the servicer.

For example, ponder the current Christian fascination with futurism, which is an expanding part of the church-growth movement. The financial side of it is only one of many aspects that needs examining, but it is an important one. After all, trend spotting has itself become a trend today—massive, fashionable, and highly lucrative. In fact, trend spotters are the fortune tellers of our world. They tell our fortunes—and make theirs.

The point is not to be insulting. Nor is it to level a charge of hypocrisy or conspiracy, as if the laudable goals were a matter of false pretense or exploitative design. The interest and the ideals are one; the masks are the face.

Yet behind the mask of care is a servicer who needs clients as much as it is a service for clients in need. Recognizing this fact is only realism in a fallen world, especially—as we are reminded ceaselessly—in a market-driven world. Unquestionably, then, Christian futurism has a powerful ideological component. Books, workshops, and audio tapes communicate ideas, but they are also extraordinary weapons for vested interests. Future-hyping and financial harvesting are closely linked. The marriage made on Wall Street will only flourish further under the influence of "the new premillenialism"—the buildup to the year 2000. How else can one explain what once-responsible Christian publishers are publishing today?

Or again, ponder the effect that the general preoccupation with marketing has on church growth. If, as its advocates claim, marketing is so important that it should be applied to every-thing, it becomes disingenuous to pretend that marketing is "neutral" or that its only dirty side is "sales."

For a start, there is an irony in the timing of the new Chris-tian enthusiasm for marketing. Just as the threats of Soviet state totalitarianism have receded, Western liberal societies are becom-ing aware of what Robert Bellah calls "market totalitarianism." Market forces are invading and colonizing more of human life, subjecting it to the constraints and criteria of money. The result is an encroaching "commodification" of everything, the reduction of the human to the economic, behavior to self-interest, wis-dom to "cost-effectiveness," success to "productivity," society to "an arena for competitive individualism," and human beings to "consumers" and "maximizers."

Examples of the marketing/maximizing mentality abound. Many Christians have grown lazy in their use of "market place" as a catch-all metaphor for public life—as if the Greek and Romans had no forum and no theatre and reduced all of public life to buying and selling. One church-growth expert judges ministers' accountability not by faithfulness but by productivity—whether "the people keep coming and giving." One national ministry advertises its ministry in explicitly self-interest terms. Its "mentorship" ministry is "realistically intended to take no more than one and one-half hours per week." Mentorship, it claims with a minimum of theology and experience and a maximum of rational choice theory, "maximizes the leverage of my greatest asset—my time. With a minimum amount of time investment I can be involved in passing on wisdom. . . as a Christian businessman."

As such examples show, marketing is far from neutral. Once summoned, it becomes a very demanding genie. As Johann Tetzel's selling of papal indulgences demonstrated in the time of Martin Luther, in the end the Midas touch of commodification turns even grace into gold.

Steps in this direction can be seen in several places today. In architecture and style, for instance, the megachurches are a gigantic mutation in the churches' age-old "edifice complex." They are the natural counterparts of megamalls, super-supermarkets, and multiplex cinemas, and resemble a cross between shopping malls and theme parks—modernity's ultimate in people-moving selling-machines. The result is "spiritual empo riums" or the "malling of religion"—grand cathedrals of consumption, one-stop church complexes premised on controlled environments with multiple-option boutiques catering to diverse needs. Through cars, their "local church" catchment area becomes citywide; through television, worldwide. Or in its public appeal, niche-marketed church growth threatens to reduce the gospel to the level of what Philip Rieff calls the "rubber nipple therapies" on the great "anxiety market."[2]

But for Christians the most important impact of marketing is always on the message itself. One church-growth marketer claims that the difference between "growth" and "evangelism" and "marketing" is only semantics. He is absolutely wrong. As historian David Potter pointed out in his penetrating analysis of advertising: once marketing becomes dominant, the concern is not with "finding an audience to hear their message but rather with finding a message to hold their audience."[3] After all, when the audience and not the message is sovereign, the good news of Jesus Christ is no longer the end, but just the means.

As a result, when megachurch pastors seek to mold a message to their "market" of constituent needs their preaching omits key components. Gone are the hard sayings of Jesus. Gone is the teaching on sin, self-denial, sacrifice, suffering, judgment, hell. With all its need-meeting emphases, there is little in the church-growth movement that stands crosswise to the world. Messianic marketing is bringing contemporary evangelicalism perilously close to the liberalism criticized earlier by Richard Niebuhr as "a God without wrath [bringing] men without sin into a Kingdom without judgement through the ministrations of a Christ without a Cross."[4]

Third, follow the bouncing ball. A common reason many people are uncritical today is that they see trends as simple, straight, and short—almost like the flight path of a missile. But in fact, trends are much more like the bounce patterns of a ball in a pinball machine. Where it comes from, where is bouncing to, and what it is hitting on the way are more important in interpreting a trend than seeing precisely where it is at any particular moment.

On the one hand, this means that we must be able to trace a trend backward and ask where it came from, and why. Unless we do so, the power of the new becomes self-evident and mesmerizing. We then become too tongue-tied to ask questions and find ourselves swept into depths of uncritical acceptance.

For example, look more closely at one of the defining features of church-growth rhetoric: what might be called its justification by contrast. We have shifted decisively, church-growth experts announce, from an era of proclamation to one of incarnation, from product-centered thinking to audience-centered thinking, from a focus on tradition to one on change, from a concern for theology to one for doing, and so on.

The rhetoric and the rationale are consciously articulated through these big contrasts, but the contrasts are rarely examined. Can they be serious, for instance, about the purported shift from proclamation to incarnation? Are we not followers of a Savior who embodied both? How can any Christian support a shift from proclamation knowing where the shift comes from — the death of the word in an image-dominant culture? Christians who know only trends, and not where they came from, will always remain uncritical. Heads may nod sagely, hands may scribble furiously, but minds will be only in neutral.

On the other hand, we must also be able to trace a trend forward and ask where it is going and with what result. The same trend that we may consider acceptable in the light of its origins may be anathema in the light of its outcome. The reason is that the opposite of bad is not necessarily good. There is an ethic of results as well as of intention. As Martin Luther warned, many of our human efforts are like those of a drunken peasant who clambers back onto his donkey only to topple off on the other side.

For example, as noted before, being "all things to all people" can be a prelude to good communication or to surprisingly self-subversion and shabby compromise. For a start, many "seeker-friendly" churches have quite deliberately subordinated both worship and discipleship to evangelism, and evangelism to entertainment, and in the process subverted the traditional defining features of the church. Further, they are blind to the dangers in the current stress on "felt needs." Their efforts might lead to one of the mightiest spiritual harvests in Christian history, but they might also lead to a bumper crop of Western "rice Christians" that makes a mockery of the gospel and of the seriousness of the hour. What does it say of the church when *Newsweek* can note that "the least demanding churches are now in greatest demand"? Or when one church can advertise: "Instead of me fitting a religion I found a religion to fit me"?[5]

Knowing how to follow the bouncing ball means that it is always wise to look for the countertrend as well as the trend, and above all to note what does not fit within the trend. That reason is likely to be the key to the old trend petering out and a new one beginning.

Fourth, check for contemporary conceit. Nothing is more characteristically modern than a repudiation of the past. In its cruder form, this disparagement grows into the silliness of a "newer-the-truer" or "latest-greatest" attitude. But even at more subdued and sophisticated levels, many modern thinkers are infected by what Thomas Oden calls "modern chauvinism."[6] Those who use the insights and tools of modernity uncritically exaggerate the newness, uniqueness, universality, and permanence of the present—and thus buy into the illusion of its truth and timelessness.

G. K. Chesterton skewered the unreflective vanity of this contemporary conceit: "A man who seriously describes his faith as Modernism might just as well invent a creed called Monday-ism, meaning that he puts special faith in the fancies that occurred to him on Monday; or a creed call Morningism; meaning that he believed in the thoughts that occurred to him in the morning and not in the afternoon."[7]

The church-growth movement is vulnerable to contemporary conceit at two main points. The first is where it underestimates the power of the present in its arguments—for example, in its reliance on futurism. George Orwell is often taken as a futurist writer because of his novel *1984*. But in fact his title was simply a reversal of the year 1948, when he wrote. He was a scathing critic of futurism. Futurism, he said, in a critique more biblical than that of most Christian futurists, is "a major mental disease of our time."

This is because futurism is based on two major fallacies. One is intellectual: what claims to be prediction is really projection ("a continuation of the thing that is happening"). The other is moral: in not questioning the projection of the status quo into the future, futurism becomes the "worship of power." Thus futurism is a form of modern chauvinism by definition. It is really a misnomer. The discipline should more accurately be called "presentism" because it is built on a license to allow the power of the present to go unchallenged. (Pop-futurist John Naisbitt at least has the candor to call himself a "Nowist.") True prophetic imagination, by contrast, is subversive because it relativizes the present and keeps it provisional. But spurious modern futurism so exaggerates the present that it overlooks all the future interventions and accidents of history— all the free acts that allow God to be God and human beings to be free.

Church growth's second vulnerable point is the reverse— where it overestimates the power of the present in its arguments. An example is the widespread attitude to the movement's capacity to "reach the unchurched." Forty-five percent of Americans are unchurched, it is widely quoted. And nothing is said to demonstrate the power and persuasive relevance of the church-growth movement more than its track record in reaching "unchurched Harrys and Marys," or "BOOMERS," understood as Believers Outside Of Most Every Religious System.

Nothing can take away from the joy in heaven over every sinner who has repented, baby boomer or otherwise. But four things must be pointed out: First, many megachurches make much of their front-door statistics (who comes and why) but less of their back-door statistics that are even more revealing (who leaves and why). Then, suddenly, like fast-growing insurance companies whose unrenewed policies exceed their new policies, they decline or collapse.

Second, a very large part of church-growth success in the West (as much as 80 percent in America, some say) is growth by transfer, not conversion. As Jim Petersen of the Navigators says: "Increase of this sort isn't church growth at all. It's just a reshuffling of the same fifty-two cards."[8]

Third, most of the "unchurched" reached would be better described as "semi-churched." Studies show that nearly half of America's "unchurched" think about going to church at least once a week—which greatly increases the chance of having people accept an invitation to church.[9] There are exceptions, such as parts of New England and the West and Northwest (less than one-fourth of the residents of Colorado, Nevada, Washington, Oregon, and Montana belong to any religious group).[10] In other words, most of the newly reached "unchurched" are really spiritual refugees from the collapse of three groups—legalistic fundamentalism, watered-down liberalism, and overritualistic traditionalism. The United States has yet to see the real unchurched as European Christians have experienced them.

Fourth, with such a memory of the gospel and such a developed sense of need, those reached recently by the church-growth movement are hardly examples of "persuasion." For all the talk of "non-traditional churches" priding themselves on "seeker-friendly" services, the result is only a jazzing up of very traditional "guest services." If the cultural drift goes on, however, real persuasion may soon be needed—of people who are closed, not open, not interested, and not needy; "unchurched Harrys and Marys" who will never darken the doors of even the most super of superchurches. If that day dawns, the unchurched will not come to us. We must leave the church and go out to them—as missionaries of Christ have always done.

Fifth, look for the overlooked. If the third and fourth tips look behind the trend to better understand the trend itself, the fifth does the same to see what will be its likely outcome. Each new trend, in other words, has a foreground and a background, headlines and small print, but the long-term strengths and weaknesses emerge from the background and the small print as much as from the more obvious side.

This point is germane to the church-growth movement because of its explicit commitment to change and innovation.

Modernity has made change its point of continuity, so any Christians who pride themselves on being innovative need to keep on asking themselves two questions.

First, in all our changes, what are we dismantling? G. K. Chesterton reminds us of the difference between constructive and destructive change, between wise reform and impatient radicalism. The impatient radical, Chesterton says, sweeps things away without a thought: "I don't see the use of it. Clear it away!"[11]

The wise reformer, on the other hand, says, "If you don't see the use of it, I won't let you clear it away. Only when you come back and say you do see the use of it, will I allow you to clear it away."

Chesterton points out the reason for prudence about change. While no human institutions are eternal, all were historical before they were social. In other words, they were created at a certain time, a certain place, and for a certain purpose—and those who forget this and treat their ancestors as fools are likely only to demonstrate that the heritage is alive and well.

Second, in all our changes, what are we repressing? The return and revenge of the repressed is a very real thing to Christians because both unbelievers and believers "hold the truth in unrighteousness." The difference is that, whereas unbelievers deny the repression and make it the center of their rebellion, believers acknowledge it and make it the center of their redemption.

Thus, just as we will be sinful until we see Christ face to face and are always more sinful than we realize, so we are also more morally and culturally short-sighted than we realize—and more foolish than we like to admit. In the revenge of the repressed, God's full reality has the last laugh even on Christian conceits.

Each of the church-growth movement's justifications by contrast carries this danger. If something new is emphasized, something old is overlooked. Yet in the long run the overlooked may be more important to the church than the emphasized. Thus few would disagree that the church-growth teaching represents a shift from the vertical dimension to the horizontal, from the theological to the practical, from the prophetic to the seeker-friendly, from the timeless to the relevant and contemporary, from the primacy of worship to the primacy of evangelism, and from the priority of Christian discipleship in all of life to the priority of spiritual ministries within the church.

But what happens when the much-heralded new emphases are seen from the standpoint of the Scriptures to be quite simply wrong? And what happens if tomorrow's "need" is for what is overlooked today? For example, what will "seeker-friendly" pastors say when the "cows of Bashan" in Beverly Hills or the "white-washed sepulchers" of Fortune 100 boardrooms require a prophetic word? Will the habitual need-meeters meet the need or will their gospel be found to have a missing note? How will we distinguish them from the need-meeting false prophets of their day?

The megachurches' disdain for theology and the seminaries is particularly striking. Anyone receiving a dime for every negative reference to theology would soon be a millionaire. Theology is said to be cerebral, theoretical, wordy, divisive, specialized, remote—an obviously unwelcome intruder to the Holy Family of the spiritual, the relational, and the practical. The success of the superchurches, it is said, is the wave of the future. The traditional seminaries and their training can be ignored. They are on their way to join the Dodo bird.

Contemporary theology, needless to say, must bear a good deal of the blame for its own rejection. Nothing, in fact, is more sobering than theology's own needed confession: Worse than management without theology is theology that is a form of attempted management—of God. The former error leads to banality, the latter to blasphemy. But even this recognition is a far cry from the fatuousness that discounts theology altogether and still expects to maintain the "church" in church growth. Because the seminaries have the potential to be the Christian equivalent of the burgeoning secular think tanks, they are on the edge of a major renaissance. At the very least, the best of them will far outlast the most celebrated of the current super-churches.

Sixth, face up to the tough tensions. The sixth tip points to a fruitful way of handling trends, which is living with their tensions.

Many Christians display an open discomfort with tension. When tensions are practical, they are seen as the root of such negatives as pressure, stress, overload, crisis, and burnout. When tensions are theological or philosophical, they are viewed as part and parcel of ambiguity, doubt, and skepticism. Tension, in short, is closer to unbelief than faith.

But this view is too pious by half and light years removed from the robust view of tension in the Scriptures. Part of the root meaning of faith in Hebrew is the concept of "tautness," just as a recurring biblical picture of sin is "slackness."

Some tensions grow out of creation—for example, the tension between divine sovereignty and human significance, and thus between action and prayer. Others grow out of the Fall—for example, our being in the world, but not of it. But the overall picture of tension is closer to the springy resilience of a trampoline than the anxieties of a high-wire act. George Whitefield captured the adventurous side of tension when he wrote in his journal, "I am never better than when I am on the full stretch for God."[12] George Macdonald conveyed the more mundane: "Our human life is often, at best, but an oscillation between the extremes which together make the truth."[13]

The challenge to faith, then, is to remember the full counsel of God and search out the different poles of the tensions to be grasped. Church-growth sociology tells us, for example, that the going trend is away from the denominational toward the local, from fixed commitments to multiple-option diversity. As *Newsweek* says, "This is the 1990s, an age of mix 'em, match 'em salad-bar spirituality. . . where brand loyalty is a doctrine of the past and the customer is king."[14]

But where this is in fact the case, one pole needs to be balanced by another, the sociology by theology. The same church that is irreducibly local is also catholic and universal. The same gospel that reaches out to shopping-consumer seekers also fixes their satisfaction on a commitment that is exclusive, final, and brooks no rival.

This principle of living with tension has always been important, but it is magnified under the conditions of modernity. If modernity represents a massive shift of the accent from the spiritual to the secular, we must consciously become deeper and more spiritual even as modernity makes us ever more knowledgeable and skilled on the secular level. Are we up-to-date in trend analysis and far-sighted through our futurism? Then how are we doing in character growth through the Sermon on the Mount? Or in spiritual nourishment through prayer, fasting, solitude, and a knowledge of the Christian classics?

If this sense of balance, tension, and opposition is lost in the craze for the relevant and the seeker-friendly, the gospel too will be lost. As Kierkegaard warned, "The Christianity of the New Testament rests upon the assumption that the Christian is in a relationship of opposition, that to be a Christian is to believe in God, to love Him, in a relationship of *opposition*. . . . In 'Christendom' we are all Christians—therefore the relationship of opposition drops out."[15]

No truth, however clearly stated, is the whole truth. No single principle, however well applied, is the all-sufficient answer. All our truths, principles, and emphases need balancing. Only so will the church demonstrate the fullness of the truth that sets us free.

Seven: Remember first things and first love. The last tip is a reminder of two elementary verities—the good is often the enemy of the best, and the sure road to unbelief is not rebellion but forgetfulness. Thus, when our skills and experience in church growth are at their highest, the first thing to say about church growth is that church growth is not the first thing.

By God's grace, modernity may confer on us a training, expertise, sophistication, and track record that would be the envy of previous generations of faith. We may even appear to have exceeded the greatest exploits of the apostles and of the times of revival. But this is still only by God's grace. We must never assuage our former anxieties with what one church-growth enthusiast described to *Time* magazine as the "self-confident Christianity" of the superchurches.

When all is said and done, what matters is not that we see Satan fall and church membership rise but that our names are written in heaven. Nothing more poignant could be said of this generation than that our church planting was illustrious but we lost our first love. There is only one real question, writes Henri Nouwen, "The question is not: How many people take you seriously? How much are you going to accomplish? Can you show some results? but: Are you in love with Jesus?"[16]

QUESTIONS FOR REFLECTION AND DISCUSSION

1. What do you think would happen if you made a habit of asking yourself in response to all speeches, sermons, books, and other communications: "What is being said? Is it true? What should be done?" (see page 74)

2. Where do you see market forces invading more and more of modern life? How about church life? (see pages 75–78)

3. Think of specific examples of constructive and destructive changes in church life. What was it that made the difference between the positive and the negative assessment? (see pages 83–84)

4. Read the opening and closing meditations by Søren Kierkegaard and Nathaniel Hawthorne from the nineteenth century. Where do you think their parables have lessons for us in the twentieth century? What do you think they might have thought of the church-growth movement?

CONCLUSION

THE CHALLENGE AT THE HEART of the church-growth movement is the problem of modern discipleship writ large—how to engage in the world of modernity freely but faithfully. Clearly, a tough blend of attributes is required: integrity and effectiveness, enterprise with humility, spiritual devotion along with common sense. To that end, here are two concluding reminders and two cautions to ponder.

The first reminder concerns the paradox surrounding change and relevance. On the one hand, no one and nothing stays the same unless they are willing to change. On the other hand, no one and nothing becomes truly timely unless they are in touch with the eternal.

The second reminder concerns the paradox surrounding success. On the one hand, in matters of the spirit, nothing fails like success. On the other hand, in matters of the spirit, nothing succeeds like failure.

The first caution to ponder is historical. In the early eighties when the Christian Right was the dominant trend, criticism of the movement was often treated as treason. Today, when the trail of its debris-strewn illusions is all too obvious, many former enthusiasts wonder why they did not recognize its shortcomings earlier. Could it be that the church-growth movement in its present expansionist phase is also a movement waiting to be undeceived? It would be wise to raise our questions now.

The second caution to ponder is theological. If modernity is history's greatest reinforcement of the idol-making factory that is our hearts, nothing can resist it short of the truth of radical monotheism: "There is one God. There is no god but God. And there is no rest for any people who have any god but God." Only an impossible God, revealing impossible truths and making impossible demands can call out an impossible people adequate for this challenge.

For all who are committed to church growth and eager to use the best of modernity, it is sobering to realize the lengths of God's iconoclasm. As the Scriptures show, God is not only against the idolizing of alien gods but he is against his own gifts when idolized. The fate of the tabernacle and the temple are both a warning to megachurches built not on rock but sand.

The attraction of a miraculous relevance that can turn stones into bread is the devil's first temptation. As Fyodor Dostoevsky depicts it in *The Brothers Karamazov*, the church with the capacity to introduce miracle, mystery, and authority without Christ is the church whose dishonor is to "correct the work of Christ" and side with the devil and the Grand Inquisitor.

We should therefore heed Origen's ancient principle: Christians are free to plunder the Egyptians, but forbidden to set up a golden calf. By all means plunder freely of the treasures of modernity, but in God's name make sure that what comes out of the fire, which will test our life's endeavors, is gold fit for the temple of God and not a late-twentieth century image of a golden calf.

We should therefore keep in mind Peter Berger's contemporary warning that they who sup with the devil of modernity had better have long spoons. By all means dine freely at the table of modernity, but in God's name keep your spoons long.

CLOSING MEDITATION

THE CELESTIAL RAIL-ROAD
Nathaniel Hawthorne

NOT A GREAT WHILE AGO, passing through the gate of dreams, I visited that region of the earth in which lies the famous city Destruction. It interested me much to learn, that, by the public spirit of some of the inhabitants, a rail-road has recently been established between this populous and flourishing town and the Celestial City. Having a little time upon my hands, I resolved to gratify a liberal curiosity by making a trip thither. Accordingly, one fine morning, after paying my bill at the hotel, and directing the porter to stow my luggage behind a coach, I took my seat in the vehicle, and set out for the Station House. It was my good fortune to enjoy the company of a gentleman—one Mr. Smooth-it-away—who, though he had never actually visited the Celestial City, yet seemed as well acquainted with its laws, customs, policy, and statistics, as with those of the city of Destruction, of which he was a native townsman. Being, moreover, a director of the rail-road corporation, and one of its largest stockholders, he had it in his power give me all desirable information respecting that praiseworthy enterprise.

Our coach rattled out of the city, and, at a short distance from its outskirts, passed over a bridge, of elegant construction, but somewhat too slight, as I imagined, to sustain any considerable weight. On both sides lay an extensive quagmire, which could not have been more disagreeable either to sight or smell, had all the kennels of the earth emptied their pollution there.

"This," remarked Mr. Smooth-it-away, "is the famous Slough of Despond—a disgrace to all the neighborhood; and greater, that it might so easily be converted into firm ground."

"I have understood," said I, "that efforts have been made for that purpose, from time immemorial. Bunyan mentions that above twenty thousand cart-loads of wholesome instructions had been thrown in here, without effect."

"Very probably!—and what effect could be anticipated from such unsubstantial stuff?" cried Mr. Smooth-it-away. "You observe this convenient bridge. We obtained a sufficient foundation for it by throwing into the slough some editions of books of morality, volumes of French philosophy and German rationalism, tracts, sermons, and essays of modern clergymen, extracts from Plato, Confucius, and various Hindoo sages, together with a few ingenious commentaries upon texts of Scripture—all of which, by some scientific process, have been converted into a mass like granite. The whole bog might be filled up with similar matter."

It really seemed to me, however, that the bridge vibrated and heaved up and down, in a very formidable manner; and, spite of Mr. Smooth-it-away's testimony to the solidity of its foundation, I should be loth to cross it in a crowded omnibus; especially if each passenger were encumbered with as heavy luggage as that gentleman and myself. Nevertheless, we got over without accident, and soon found ourselves at the Station House. This very neat and spacious edifice is erected on the site of the little Wicket-Gate, which formerly, as all old pilgrims will recollect, stood directly across the highway, and, by its inconvenient narrowness, was a great obstruction to the traveller of liberal mind and expansive stomach. The reader of John Bunyan will be glad to know, that Christian's old friend, Evangelist, who was accustomed to supply each pilgrim with a mystic roll, now presides at the ticket-office. Some malicious persons, it is true, deny the identity of this reputable character with the Evangelist of old times, and even pretend to bring competent evidence of an imposture. Without involving myself in the dispute, I shall merely observe, that, so far as my experience goes, the square pieces of pasteboard, now delivered to passengers, are much more convenient and useful along the road, than the antique roll of parchment. Whether they will be as readily received at the gate of the Celestial City, I decline giving an opinion.

A large number of passengers were already at the Station House, awaiting the departure of the cars. By the aspect and demeanor of these persons, it was easy to judge that the feelings of the community had undergone a very favorable change, in reference to the Celestial pilgrimage. It would have done Bunyan's heart good to see it. Instead of a lonely and ragged man, with a huge burthen on his back, plodding along sorrowfully on foot, while the whole city hooted after him, here were parties of the first gentry and most respectable people in the neighborhood, setting forth towards the Celestial City, as cheerfully as if the pilgrimage were merely a summer tour. Among the gentlemen were characters of deserved eminence, magistrates, politicians, and men of wealth, by whose example religion could not but be greatly recommended to their meaner brethren. In the ladies' apartment, too, I rejoiced to distinguish some of those flowers of fashionable society, who are so well fitted to adorn the most elevated circles of the Celestial City. There was much pleasant conversation about the news of the day, topics of business, politics, or the lighter matters of amusement; while religion, though indubitably the main thing at heart, was thrown tastefully into the back-ground. Even an infidel would have heard little or nothing to shock his sensibility.

One great convenience of the new method of going on pilgrimage, I must not forget to mention. Our enormous burthens, instead of being carried on our shoulders, as had been the custom of old, were all snugly deposited in the baggage-car, and, as I was assured, would be delivered to their respective owners, at the journey's end. Another thing, likewise the benevolent reader will be delighted to understand. It may be remembered that there was an ancient feud between Prince Beelzebub and the keeper of

the Wicket-Gate, and that the adherents of the former distinguished personage were accustomed to shoot deadly arrows at
honest pilgrims, while knocking at the door. This dispute, much
to the credit as well of the illustrious potentate above-mentioned
as of the worthy and enlightened Directors of the rail-road, has
been pacifically arranged, on the principle of mutual compromise. The prince's subjects are now pretty numerously employed
about the Station House, some in taking care of the baggage,
others in collecting fuel, feeding the engines, and such congenial
occupations; and I can conscientiously affirm, that persons more
attentive to their business, more willing to accommodate, or
more generally agreeable to the passengers, are not to be found
on any rail-road. Every good heart must surely exult at so satis-
factory an arrangement of an immemorial difficulty.

"Where is Mr. Greatheart?" inquired I. "Beyond a doubt,
the Directors have engaged that famous old champion to be
chief engineer on the rail-road?"

"Why, no," said Mr. Smooth-it-away, with a dry cough: "He
was offered the situation of brake-man; but, to tell you the truth,
our friend Greatheart has grown preposterously stiff and narrow,
in his old age. He has so often guided pilgrims over the road, on
foot, that he considers it a sin to travel in any other fashion.
Besides, the old fellow had entered so heartily into the ancient
feud with Prince Beelzebub, that he would have been perpetually
at blows or ill language with some of the prince's subjects, and
thus have embroiled us anew. So, on the whole, we were not
sorry when honest Greatheart went off to the Celestial City in a
huff, and left us at liberty to choose a more suitable and accom-
modating man. Yonder comes the engineer of the train. You will
probably recognize him at once."

The engine at this moment took its station in advance of
the cars, looking, I must confess, much more like a sort of
mechanical demon, that would hurry us to the infernal regions,
than a laudable contrivance for smoothing our way to the Celestial City. On its top sat a personage almost enveloped in smoke
and flame, which—not to startle the reader—appeared to gush

from his own mouth and stomach, as well as from the engine's brazen abdomen.

"Do my eyes deceive me?" cried I. "What on earth is this! A living creature?—if so, he is own brother to the engine that he rides upon!"

"Poh, poh; you are obtuse!" said Mr. Smooth-it-away, with a hearty laugh. "Don't you know Apollyon, Christian's old enemy with whom he fought so fierce a battle in the Valley of Humiliation? He was the very fellow to manage the engine; and so we have reconciled him to the custom of going on pilgrimage, and engaged him as chief engineer."

"Bravo, bravo!" exclaimed I, with irrepressible enthusiasm. "This shows the liberality of the age; this proves, if anything can, that all musty prejudices are in a fair way to be obliterated. And how will Christian rejoice to hear of this happy transformation of his old antagonist! I promise myself great pleasure in informing him of it, when we reach the Celestial City."

The passengers being all comfortably seated, we now rattled away merrily, accomplishing a greater distance in ten minutes, than Christian probably trudged over, in a day. It was laughable, while we glanced along, as it were, at the tail of a thunder-bolt, to observe two dusty foot-travellers, in the old pilgrim-guise, with cockle-shell and staff, their mystic rolls of parchment in their hands, and their intolerable burthens on their backs. The preposterous obstinacy of these honest people in persisting to groan and stumble along the difficult pathway, rather than take advantage of modern improvements, excited great mirth among our wiser brotherhood. We greeted the two pilgrims with many pleasant gibes and a roar of laughter; whereupon, they gazed at us with such woeful and absurdly compassionate visages, that our merriment grew tenfold more obstreperous. Apollyon, also, entered heartily into the fun, and contrived to flirt the smoke and flame of the engine, or of his own breath, into their faces, and enveloped them in an atmosphere of scalding steam. These little practical jokes amused us mightily, and doubtless afforded the pilgrims the gratification of considering themselves martyrs.

At some distance from the rail-road, Mr. Smooth-it-away pointed to a large, antique edifice, which, he observed, was a tavern of long standing, and had formerly been a noted stopping-place for pilgrims. In Bunyan's road-book, it is mentioned as the Interpreter's House.

"I have long had a curiosity to visit that old mansion," remarked I.

"It is not one of our stations, as you perceive," said my companion. "The keeper was violently opposed to the rail-road and well he might be, as the track left his house of entertainment on one side, and thus was pretty certain to deprive him of all his reputable customers. But the foot-path still passes his door; and the old gentleman now and then receives a call from some simple traveller, and entertains him with fare as old-fashioned as himself."

Before our talk on this subject came to a conclusion, we were rushing by the place where Christian's burthen fell from his shoulders, at the sight of the cross. This served as a theme for Mr. Smooth-it-away, Mr. Live-for-the-world, Mr. Hide-sin-in-the-heart, Mr. Scaly Conscience, and a knot of gentlemen from the town Shun Repentance, to descant upon the inestimable advantages resulting from the safety of our baggage. Myself, and all the passengers indeed, joined with great unanimity in this view of the matter; for our burthens were rich in many things, esteemed precious throughout the world; and, especially, we each of us possessed a great variety of favorite Habits, which we trusted would not be out of fashion, even in the polite circles of the Celestial City. It would have been a sad spectacle, to see such an assortment of valuable articles tumbling into the sepulchre. Thus pleasantly conversing on the favorable circumstances of our position, as compared with those of past pilgrims, and of narrow-minded ones at the present day, we soon found ourselves at the foot of the Hill Difficulty. Through the very heart of this rocky mountain a tunnel has been constructed, of most admirable architecture, with a lofty arch and a spacious double-track; so that, unless the earth and rocks should chance to crumble down, it will remain an eternal monument of the builder's skill and enterprise. It is a great, though incidental advantage, that the materials from the heart of the Hill Difficulty have been employed in filling up the Valley of Humiliation; thus obviating the necessity of descending into that disagreeable and unwholesome hollow.

"This is a wonderful improvement, indeed," said I. "Yet I should have been glad of an opportunity to visit the Palace Beautiful, and be introduced to the charming young ladies—Miss Prudence, Miss Piety, Miss Charity, and the rest—who have the kindness to entertain pilgrims there."

"Young ladies!" cried Mr. Smooth-it-away, as soon as he could speak for laughing. "And charming young ladies! Why, my dear fellow, they are old maids, every soul of them—prim, starched, dry, and angular—and not one of them, I will venture to say, has altered so much as the fashion of her gown, since the days of Christian's pilgrimage."

"Ah, well," said I, much comforted. "Then I can very readily dispense with their acquaintance."

The respectable Apollyon was now putting on the steam at a prodigious rate, anxious, perhaps, to get rid of the unpleasant reminiscences connected with the spot where he had so disastrously encountered Christian. Consulting Mr. Bunyan's road-book, I perceived that we must now be within a few miles of the Valley of the Shadow of Death; into which doleful region, at our present speed, we should plunge much sooner than seemed at all desirable. In truth, I expected nothing better than to find myself in the ditch on one side, or the quag on the other. But, on communicating my apprehensions to Mr. Smooth-it-away, he assured me that the difficulties of this passage, even in its worst condition, had been vastly exaggerated, and that, in its present state of improvement, I might consider myself as safe as on any rail-road in Christendom.

Even while we were speaking, the train shot into the entrance of this dreaded Valley. Though I plead guilty to some foolish palpitations of the heart, during our headlong rush over

the causeway here constructed, yet it were unjust to withhold
the highest encomiums on the boldness of its original concep-
tion, and the ingenuity of those who executed it. It was gratify-
ing, likewise, to observe how much care had been taken to dispel
the everlasting gloom, and supply the defect of cheerful sunshine; not a ray of which has ever penetrated among these awful
shadows. For this purpose, the inflammable gas, which exudes
plentifully from the soil, is collected by means of pipes, and
thence communicated to a quadruple row of lamps, along the
whole extent of the passage. Thus a radiance has been created,
even out of the fiery and sulphurous curse that rests forever upon
the Valley; a radiance hurtful, however, to the eyes, and somewhat bewildering as I discovered by the changes which it
wrought in the visages of my companions. In this respect, as
compared with natural daylight, there is the same difference as
between truth and falsehood; but, if the reader have ever trav-
elled through the Dark Valley, he will have learned to be thank-
ful for any light that he could get; if not from the sky above,
then from the blasted soil beneath. Such was the red brilliancy of
these lamps, that they appeared to build walls of fire on both
sides of the track, between which we held our course at light-
ning-speed, while a reverberating thunder filled the Valley with
its echoes. Had the engine run off the track—a catastrophe, it is
whispered, by no means unprecedented—the bottomless pit, if
there be any such place, would undoubtedly have received us.
Just as some dismal fooleries of this nature had made my heart
quake, there came a tremendous shriek, careering along the Valley as if a thousand devils had burst their lungs to utter it, but
which proved to be merely the whistle of the engine, on arriving
at a stopping-place.

The spot, where we had now paused, is the same that our
friend Bunyan—a truthful man, but infected with many fantas-
tic notions—has designated, in terms plainer than I like to
repeat, as the mouth of the infernal region. This, however, must
be a mistake; inasmuch as Mr. Smooth-it-away, while we
remained in the smoky and lurid cavern, took occasion to prove

that Tophet has not even a metaphorical existence. The place, he assured us, is no other than the crater of a half-extinct volcano, in which the Directors had caused forges to be set up, for the manufacture of rail-road iron. Hence, also, is obtained a plentiful supply of fuel for the use of the engines. Whoever had gazed into the dismal obscurity of the broad cavern-mouth, whence, ever and anon, darted huge tongues of dusky flame,— and had seen the strange, half-shaped monsters, and visions of faces horribly grotesque, into which the smoke seemed to wreathe itself,—and had heard the awful murmurs, and shrieks, and deep shuddering whispers of the blast, sometimes forming itself into words almost articulate,—he would have seized upon Mr. Smooth-it-away's comfortable explanation, as greedily as we did. The inhabitants of the cavern, moreover, were unlovely personages, dark, smoke-begrimed, generally deformed, with misshapen feet, and a glow of dusky redness in their eyes; as if their hearts had caught fire, and were blazing out of the upper windows. It struck me as a peculiarity, that the laborers at the forge, and those who brought fuel to the engine, when they began to draw short breath, positively emitted smoke from their mouth and nostrils.

Among the idlers about the train, most of whom were puffing cigars which they had lighted at the flame of the crater, I was perplexed to notice several, who, to my certain knowledge, had heretofore set forth by rail-road for the Celestial City. They looked dark, wild, and smoky, with a singular resemblance, indeed, to the native inhabitants; like whom, also, they had a disagreeable propensity to ill-natured gibes and sneers; the habit of which had wrought a settled contortion of their visages. Having been on speaking terms with one of these persons—an indolent, good-for-nothing fellow, who went by the name of Take-it-easy—I called to him, and inquired what was his business there.

"Did you not start," said I, "for the Celestial City?"

"That's a fact," said Mr. Take-it-easy, carelessly puffing some smoke into my eyes. "But I heard such bad accounts, that I never took pains to climb the hill, on which the city stands. No business doing—no fun going on—nothing to drink, and no smoking allowed—and a thrumming of church-music from morning till night! I would not stay in such a place, if they offered me house-room and living free."

"But, my good Mr. Take-it-easy," cried I, "why take up your residence here, of all places in the world?"

"Oh," said the loafer, with a grin, "it is very warm hereabouts, and I meet with plenty of old acquaintances, and altogether the place suits me. I hope to see you back again, some day soon. A pleasant journey to you!"

While he was speaking, the bell of the engine rang, and we dashed away, after dropping a few passengers, but receiving no new ones. Rattling onward through the Valley, we were dazzled with the fiercely gleaming gas-lamps, as before. But sometimes, in the dark of intense brightness, grim faces, that bore the aspect and expression of individual sins, or evil passions, seemed to thrust themselves through the veil of light, glaring upon us, and stretching forth a great dusky hand, as if to impede our progress. I almost thought, that they were my own sins that appalled me there. These were freaks of imagination—nothing more, certainly,—mere delusions, which I ought to be heartily ashamed of—but, all through the Dark Valley, I was tormented, and pestered, and dolefully bewildered, with the same kind of waking dreams. The mephitic gasses of that region intoxicate the brain. As the light of natural day, however, began to struggle with the glow of the lanterns, these vain imaginations lost their vividness, and finally vanished with the first ray of sunshine that greeted our escape from the Valley of the Shadow of Death. Ere we had gone a mile beyond it, I could well nigh have taken my oath that this whole gloomy passage was a dream.

At the end of the Valley, as John Bunyan mentions, is a cavern, where, in his days, dwelt two cruel giants, Pope and Pagan, who had strewn the ground about their residence with the bones of slaughtered pilgrims. These vile old troglodytes are no longer there; but into their deserted cave another terrible giant has

87558

thrust himself, and makes it his business to seize upon honest travellers, and fat them for his table with plentiful meals of smoke, mist, moonshine, raw potatoes, and saw-dust. He is a German by birth, and is called Giant Transcendentalist; but as to his form, his features, his substance, and his nature generally, it is the chief peculiarity of this huge miscreant, that neither he for himself, nor anybody for him, has ever been able to describe them. As we rushed by the cavern's mouth, we caught a hasty glimpse of him, looking somewhat like an ill-proportioned figure, but considerably more like a heap of fog and duskiness. He shouted after us, but in so strange a phraseology that we knew not what he meant, nor whether to be encouraged or affrighted.

It was late in the day, when the train thundered into the ancient city of Vanity, where Vanity Fair is still at the height of prosperity, and exhibits an epitome of whatever is brilliant, gay, and fascinating, beneath the sun. As I purposed to make a considerable stay here, it gratified me to learn that there is no longer the want of harmony between the townspeople and pilgrims, which impelled the former to such lamentably mistaken measures as the persecution of Christian, and the fiery martyrdom of Faithful. On the contrary, as the new rail-road brings with it great trade and a constant influx of strangers, the lord of Vanity Fair is its chief patron, and the capitalists of the city are among the largest stockholders. Many passengers stop to take their pleasure or make their profit in the Fair, instead of going onward to the Celestial City. Indeed, such are the charms of the place, that people often affirm it to be the true and only heaven; stoutly contending that there is no other, that those who seek further are mere dreamers, and that, in the fabled brightness of the Celestial City lay but a bare mile beyond the gates of Vanity, they would not be fools enough to go thither. Without subscribing to these, perhaps, exaggerated encomiums, I can truly say, that my abode in the city was mainly agreeable, and my intercourse with the inhabitants productive of much amusement and instruction.

Being naturally of a serious turn, my attention was directed to the solid advantages derivable from a residence here, rather than to the effervescent pleasures, which are the grand object with too many visitants. The Christian reader, if he have had no accounts of the city later than Bunyan's time, will be surprised to hear that almost every street has its church, and that the reverend clergy are nowhere held in higher respect than at Vanity Fair. And well do they deserve such honorable estimation; for the maxims of wisdom and virtue, which fall from their lips, come from as deep a spiritual source, and tend to us as lofty a religious aim, as those of the sagest philosophers of old. In justification of this high praise, I need only mention the names of the Rev. Mr. Shallow-deep; the Rev. Mr. Stumble-at-truth; that fine old clerical character, the Rev. Mr. This-to-day, who expects shortly to resign his pulpit to the Rev. Mr. That-to-morrow; together with the Rev. Mr. Bewilderment; the Rev. Mr. Clog-the-spirit; and, last and greatest, the Rev. Dr. Wind-of-doctrine. The labors of these eminent divines are aided by those of innumerable lecturers, who diffuse such a various profundity, in all subjects of human or celestial science, that any man may acquire an omnigenous erudition, without the trouble of even learning to read. Thus literature is etherealized by assuming for its medium the human voice: and knowledge, depositing all its heavier particles—except, doubtless, its gold—becomes exhaled into a sound, which forthwith steals into the ever-open ear of the community. These ingenious methods constitute a sort of machinery, by which thought and study are done to every person's hand, without his putting himself to the slightest inconvenience in the matter. There is another species of machine for the wholesale manufacture of individual morality. This excellent result is effected by societies for all manner of virtuous purposes; with which a man has merely to connect himself, throwing, as it were, his quota of virtue into the common stock; and the president and directors will take care that the aggregate amount be well applied. All these, and other wonderful improvements in ethics, religion, and literature, being made plain to my comprehension by the ingenious Mr. Smooth-it-away, inspired me with a vast admiration of Vanity Fair.

It would fill a volume, in an age of pamphlets, were I to record all my observations in this great capital of human business and pleasure. There was an unlimited range of society—the powerful, the wise, the witty, and the famous in every walk of life—princes, presidents, poets, generals, artists, actors, and philanthropists, all making their own market at the Fair, and deeming no price too exorbitant for such commodities as hit their fancy. It was well worth one's while, even if he had no idea of buying or selling, to loiter through the bazaars, and observe the various sorts of traffic that were going forward.

Some of the purchasers, I thought, made very foolish bargains. For instance, a young man, having inherited a splendid fortune, laid out a considerable portion of it in the purchase of diseases, and finally spent all the rest for a heavy lot of repentance and a suit of rags. A very pretty girl bartered a heart as clear as crystal, and which seemed her most valuable possession, for another jewel of the same kind, but so worn and defaced as to be utterly worthless. In one shop, there were a great many crowns of laurel and myrtle, which soldiers, authors, statesmen, and various other people, pressed eagerly to buy; some purchased these paltry wreaths with their lives; others by a toilsome servitude of years; and many sacrificed whatever was most valuable, yet finally slunk away without the crown. There was a sort of stock or scrip, called Conscience, which seemed to be in great demand, and would purchase almost anything. Indeed, few rich commodities were to be obtained without paying a heavy sum in this particular stock; and a man's business was seldom very lucrative, unless he knew precisely when and how to throw his hoard of Conscience into the market. Yet, as this stock was the only thing of permanent value, whoever parted with it was sure to find himself a loser, in the long run. Several of the speculations were of a questionable character. Occasionally, a member of congress recruited his pocket by the sale of his constituents; and I was assured that public officers have often sold their country, at very moderate prices. Thousands sold their happiness for a whim. Gilded chains were in great demand, and purchased with almost any sacrifice.

In truth, those who desired, according to the old adage, to sell anything valuable for a song, might find customers all over the Fair; and there were innumerable messes of pottage, piping hot, for such as chose to buy them with their birth-rights. A few articles, however, could not be found genuine, at Vanity Fair. If a customer wished to renew his stock of youth, the dealers offered him a set of false teeth and an auburn wig; if he demanded peace of mind, they recommended opium or a brandy-bottle.

Tracts of land and golden mansions, situated in the Celestial City, were often exchanged, at very disadvantageous rates, for a few years lease of small, dismal, inconvenient tenements in Vanity Fair. Prince Beelzebub himself took great interest in this sort of traffic, and sometimes condescended to meddle with smaller matters. I once had the pleasure to see him bargaining with a miser for his soul, which, after much ingenious skirmishing on both sides, his Highness succeeded in obtaining at about the value of sixpence. The prince remarked, with a smile, that he was a loser by the transaction.

Day after day, as I walked the streets of Vanity, my manners and deportment became more and more like those of the inhabitants. The place began to seem like home; the idea of pursuing my travels to the Celestial City was almost obliterated from my mind. I was reminded of it however, by the sight of the same pair of simple pilgrims at whom we had laughed so heartily, when Apollyon puffed smoke and steam into their faces, at the commencement of our journey. There they stood amid the densest bustle of Vanity—the dealers offering them their purple, and fine linen, and jewels; the men of wit and humor gibing at them; a pair of buxom ladies ogling them askance; while the benevolent Mr. Smooth-it-away whispered some of his wisdom at their elbows, and pointed to a newly erected temple—but there were these worthy simpletons, making the scene look wild and monstrous, merely by their sturdy repudiation of all part in its business or pleasures.

One of them—his name was Stick-to-the-right—perceived in my face, I suppose, a species of sympathy and almost admiration, which, to my own great surprise, I could not help feeling for this pragmatic couple. It prompted him to address me.

"Sir," inquired he, with a sad, yet mild and kindly voice, "do you call yourself a Pilgrim?"

"Yes," I replied. "My right to that appellation is indubitable. I am merely a sojourner here in Vanity Fair, being bound for the Celestial City, by the new rail-road."

"Alas, friend," rejoined Mr. Stick-to-the-right, "I do assure you, and beseech you to receive the truth of my words, that that whole concern is a bubble. You may travel on it all your life-time, were you to live thousands of years, and yet never get beyond the limits of Vanity Fair! Yea; though you should deem yourself entering the gates of the Blessed City, it will be nothing but a miserable delusion."

"The Lord of the Celestial City," began the other pilgrim, whose name was Mr. Foot-it-to-Heaven, "has refused, and will ever refuse, to grant an act of incorporation for this rail-road; and unless that be obtained, no passenger can ever hope to enter his dominions. Wherefore, every man, who buys a ticket, must lay his account with losing the purchase-money—which is the value of his own soul."

"Poh, nonsense!" said Mr. Smooth-it-away, taking my arm and leading me off. "These fellows ought to be indicted for a libel. If the law stood as it once did in Vanity Fair, we should see them grinning through the iron-bars of the prison-window."

This incident made a considerable impression on my mind, and contributed with other circumstances to indispose me to a permanent residence in the city of Vanity; although, of course, I was not simple enough to give up my original plan of gliding along easily and commodiously by rail-road. Still, I grew anxious to be gone. There was one strange thing that troubled me; amid the occupations or amusements of the Fair, nothing was more common than for a person—whether at a feast, theatre, or church, or trafficking for wealth and honors, or whatever he might be doing, and however unseasonable the interruption—suddenly to vanish like a soap-bubble, and be never more seen of

his fellows; and so accustomed were the latter to such little accidents, that they went on with their business, as quietly as if nothing had happened. But it was otherwise with me.

Finally, after a pretty long residence at the Fair, I resumed
my journey towards the Celestial City, still with Mr. Smooth-
it-away at my side. At a short distance beyond the suburbs of
Vanity, we passed the ancient silver-mine, of which Demas was
the first discoverer, and which is now wrought to great advantage,
supplying nearly all the coined currency of the world. A little
further onward was the spot where Lot's wife had stood for ages,
under the semblance of a pillar of salt. Curious travellers have
long since carried it away piece-meal. Had all regrets been pun-
ished as rigorously as this poor dame's were, my yearning for the
relinquished delights of Vanity Fair might have produced a similar change in my own corporeal substance, and left me a warning to future pilgrims.

The next remarkable object was a large edifice, constructed
of moss-grown stone, but in a modern and airy style of architecture. The engine came to a pause in its vicinity, with the usual
tremendous shriek.

"This was formerly the castle of the redoubted giant Despair,"
observed Mr. Smooth-it-away; "but, since his death, Mr. Flimsy-
faith has repaired it, and now keeps an excellent house of entertainment here. It is one of our stopping-places."

"It seems but slightly put together," remarked I, looking at
the frail, yet ponderous walls. "I do not envy Mr. Flimsy-faith
his habitation. Some day, it will thunder down upon the heads of
the occupants."

"We shall escape, at all events," said Mr. Smooth-it-away;
"for Apollyon is putting on the steam again."

The road now plunged into a gorge of the Delectable Moun-
tains, and traversed the field where, in former ages, the blind
men wandered and stumbled among the tombs. One of these
ancient tomb-stones had been thrust across the track, by some
malicious person, and gave the train of cars a terrible jolt. Far
up the rugged side of a mountain, I perceived a rusty iron-door,

half-overgrown with bushes and creeping-plants, but with smoke issuing from its crevices.

"Is that," inquired I, "the very door in the hill-side, which the shepherds assured Christian was a by-way to hell?"

"That was a joke on the part of the shepherds," said Mr. Smooth-it-away, with a smile. "It is neither more nor less than the door of a cavern, which they use as a smoke-house for the preparation of mutton-hams."

My recollections of the journey are now, for a little space, dim and confused; inasmuch as a singular drowsiness here overcame me, owing to the fact that we were passing over the Enchanted Ground, the air of which encourages a disposition to sleep. I awoke, however, as soon as we crossed the borders of the pleasant land of Beulah. All the passengers were rubbing their eyes, comparing watches, and congratulating one another on the prospect of arriving so seasonably at the journey's end. The sweet breezes of this happy clime came refreshingly to our nostrils; we beheld the glimmering gush of silver fountains, overhung by trees of beautiful foliage and delicious fruit, which were propagated by grafts from the Celestial gardens. Once, as we dashed onward like a hurricane, there was a flutter of wings, and the bright appearance of an angel in the air, speeding forth on some heavenly mission. The engine now announced the close vicinity of the final Station House, by one last and horrible scream, in which there seemed to be distinguishable every kind of wailing and woe, and bitter fierceness of wrath, all mixed up with the wild laughter of a devil or a madman. Throughout our journey, at every stopping-place, Apollyon had exercised his ingenuity in screwing the most abominable sounds out of the whistle of the steam-engine; but, in this closing effort, he outdid himself, and created an infernal uproar, which, besides disturbing the peaceful inhabitants of Beulah, must have sent its discord even through the Celestial gates.

While the horrid clamor was still ringing in our ears, we heard an exulting strain, as if a thousand instruments of music, with height, and depth, and sweetness in their tones, at once tender and triumphant, were struck in unison, to greet the approach of some illustrious hero, who had fought the good fight, and won a glorious victory, and was come to lay aside his battered arms forever. Looking to ascertain what might be the occasion of this glad harmony, I perceived, on alighting from the cars, that a multitude of Shining Ones had assembled on the other side of the river, to welcome two poor pilgrims, who were just emerging from its depths. They were the same whom Apollyon and ourselves had persecuted with taunts and gibes, and scalding steam, at the commencement of our journey; the same whose unworldly aspect and impressive words had stirred my conscience, amid the wild revellers of Vanity Fair.

"How amazingly well those men have got on!" cried I to Mr. Smooth-it-away. "I wish we were secure of as good a reception."

"Never fear—never fear!" answered my friend. "Come!—make haste!—the ferry-boat will be off directly; and in three minutes you will be on the other side of the river. No doubt you will find coaches to carry you up to the city-gates."

A steam ferry-boat, the last improvement on this important route, lay at the river-side, puffing, snorting, and emitting all those other disagreeable utterances, which betoken the departure to be immediate. I hurried on board, with the rest of the passengers, most of whom were in great perturbation; some bawling out for their baggage; some tearing their hair, and exclaiming that the boat would explode or sink; some already pale with the heaving of the stream; some gazing affrighted at the ugly aspect of the steersman; and some still dizzy with the slumberous influences of the Enchanted Ground. Looking back to the shore, I was amazed to discern Mr. Smooth-it-away, waving his hand in token of farewell!

"Don't you go over to the Celestial City?" exclaimed I.

"Oh, no!" answered he with a queer smile, and that same disagreeable contortion of visage, which I had remarked in the inhabitants of the Dark Valley. "Oh, no! I have come thus far only for the sake of your pleasant company. Good bye! We shall meet again."

And then did my excellent friend, Mr. Smooth-it-away,
laugh outright; in the midst of which cachinnation, a smoke-
wreath issued from his mouth and nostrils; while a twinkle of
lurid flame darted out of either eye, proving indubitably that his
heart was all of a red blaze. The impudent Fiend! To deny the
existence of Tophet, when he felt its fiery tortures raging within
his breast! I rushed to the side of the boat, intending to fling
myself on shore. But the wheels, as they began their revolutions,
threw a dash of spray over me, so cold—so deadly cold, with the
chill that will never leave those waters, until Death be drowned
in his own river—that, with a shiver and a heart-quake, I awoke.
Thank Heaven, it was a Dream!

NOTES

INTRODUCTION

1. Jim Klobuchar, "You Can Get it All at the Megamall—Even Religion," Minneapolis *Star Tribune*, 31 August 1992, p. 3B.
2. See C. Peter Wagner, *Your Church Can Grow* (Glendale, Calif.: Regal, 1976), chapter 1, author's emphasis.
3. C. S. Lewis, *The Weight of Glory* (Grand Rapids, Mich.: Eerdmans, 1965), p. 12.
4. Leith Anderson, *Dying for Change* (Minneapolis: Bethany House, 1990), p. 17.
5. Quoted in Robert Johnson, "Preaching a Gospel of Acquisitiveness," *Wall Street Journal*, 11 December 1990, p. A4.
6. See Nathan O. Hatch, *The Democratization of American Christianity* (New Haven, Conn.: Yale University Press, 1989).
7. James D. Berkley, "Church Growth Comes of Age," *Leadership*, Fall 1991, p. 115.
8. C. S. Lewis, *George Macdonald: An Anthology* (London: Geoffrey Bles, 1946), p. 27.
9. Peter L. Berger, *A Rumor of Angels* (New York: Anchor, 1990), p. 24–25.
10. Friedrich Nietzsche, *Twilight of the Idols/The Anti-Christ* (London: Penguin, 1968), p. 21.

ONE MAIN QUESTION

1. Lewis, *George Macdonald: An Anthology*, p. 74.
2. *Publishers Weekly*, 10 February 1992, p. 42.

3. Jack Sims in Brad Edmondson, "Bringing in the Sheaves," *American Demographics*, August 1988, p. 57.
4. "The Door Interviews Michael Been," *The Door*, July/August 1991, p. 8.

THREE MAIN DANGERS OF MODERNITY

1. Philip Rieff, *The Feeling Intellect* (Chicago: University of Chicago, 1990), p. 280.
2. Pierre Bordieu, *Algeria 1960* (Cambridge: Cambridge University Press, 1979), p. 15.
3. These figures are based on an analysis of 434 essays that appeared in *Leadership Journal* between 1980 and 1988. For an extended analysis, see David F. Wells, "Things Fall Apart," chapter 3 in *No Place for Truth* (Grand Rapids, Mich.: Eerdmans, 1993).
4. Quoted in T. J. Jackson Lears, *No Place of Grace* (New York: Pantheon, 1981), p. 24.
5. William Adams Brown, vol. 1 of *The Education of American Ministers* (New York: Institute of Social and Religious Research, 1934), p. 21.
6. *Church Planning Inventory: Comparative Tabulations; 72 Congregations* (Hartford: Hartford Seminary Center for Social and Religious Research, 1986), p. 6.

FOUR MAIN STEPS IN COMPROMISE

1. George Tyrell, *Christianity at the Crossroads* (London: Allen and Unwin, 1963), p. 49.
2. Quoted in *Context*, 15 April 1991, p. 4.

FIVE MAIN IRONIES

1. Friedrich Nietzsche, *Untimely Meditations* (Cambridge: Cambridge University Press, 1983), p. 74.
2. G. K. Chesterton, "The Catholic Church and Conversion" in *Robert Knille, As I Was Saying: A Chesterton Reader* (Grand Rapids, Mich.: Eerdmans, 1985), p. 272.
3. Henri J. M. Nouwen, *In the Name of Jesus: Reflections on Christian Leadership* (New York: Crossroad, 1989), p. 17.

4. George Macdonald, *Unspoken Sermons: Second Series* (Eureka, Calif.: Sunrise Books, 1989), p. 66.
5. Ivan Illich, *Disabling Professions* (London: Marion Boyars, 1977), p. 72.
6. Clayton Carlson, quoted in William Griffin, "Decatrends," *Publishers Weekly*, 10 February 1992, p. 29; emphasis mine.
7. George Macdonald, *Unspoken Sermons*, p. 38.
8. Ibid., p. 50.

SIX MAIN CARRIERS OF MODERNITY

1. See Christopher Lasch, *The Culture of Narcissism* (New York: Warner Books, 1979) and Illich, *Disabling Professions*.

SEVEN MAIN TIPS FOR DISCERNMENT

1. Robert J. Samuelson, "The Numskull Factor," *Washington Post*, 26 June 1991, p. A19.
2. Philip Rieff, *The Feeling Intellect* (Chicago: University of Chicago Press, 1990), p. 359.
3. David M. Potter, *People of Plenty* (Chicago: University of Chicago Press, 1954), p. 154.
4. H. Richard Niebuhr, *The Kingdom of God in America* (New York: Harper Torchback), p. 191–92.
5. Kenneth L. Woodward, "A Time to Seek," *Newsweek*, 17 December 1990, p. 56.
6. Thomas C. Oden, "On Not Whoring After the Spirit of the Age, in Os Guinness and John Seel, eds., *No God But God: Breaking With the Idols of Our Age* (Chicago: Moody Press, 1992), p. 193.
7. G. K. Chesterton, "The New Case for Catholic Schools," in *Knille, As I Was Saying*, p. 178.
8. Jim Petersen, *Church Without Walls* (Colorado Springs: NavPress, 1992), p. 111.
9. See *Context*, 1 December 1991, p. 5.
10. "Go West, Young Man," *National and International Religion Report*, Vol. 6, No. 16, 27 July 1992.
11. G. K. Chesterton, "The Drift from Domesticity," in *Knille, As I Was Saying*, p. 127.
12. George Whitefield, *Journals* (London: The Banner of Truth Trust, 1960), p. 136.

13. George Macdonald, "One Reason for Sex" in Lewis, *George Macdonald: An Anthology*, p. 105.
14. Woodward, "A Time to Seek," p. 50.
15. Søren Kierkegaard, *Kierkegaard's Attack Upon "Christendom,"* trans. Walter Lowrie (Princeton: Princeton University Press, 1968), p. 149.
16. Nouwen, *In the Name of Jesus*, p. 24.

254.5
G9647
c.1

87558

254.5 G9647 c.1
Guinness, Os.
Dining with the devil

DEMCO